LOW-CALORIE

CAJUN

· COOKING ·

Enola Prudhomme's

LOW-CALORIE CAJUN COOKING

Illustrations by
Barry Zaid

◆

Hearst Books
New York

For Mom, who taught me how to cook. Dad, for teaching me the values of life. My late brother-in-law Saul Broussard and my late nephew Russell Prudhomme, Jr.

Copyright © 1991 by Enola Prudhomme

Recognizing the importance of preserving what has been written, it is the policy of William Morrow and Company, Inc., and its imprints and affiliates to have the books it publishes printed on acid-free paper, and we exert our best efforts to that end.

Library of Congress Cataloging-in-Publication Data
Prudhomme, Enola.
    [Low-calorie Cajun cooking]
    Enola Prudhomme's low-calorie Cajun cooking.
        p.   cm.
    Includes index.
    ISBN 0-688-09255-1
    1. Cookery, Cajun.   2. Low-calorie diet—Recipes.
    I. Title.   II. Title: Low-calorie Cajun cooking.
    TX715.P9478   1991
    641.59763—dc20   90-5244
                                                        CIP

Printed in the United States of America

First Edition

6 7 8 9 10

BOOK DESIGN BY BARRY ZAID

CONTENTS

ACKNOWLEDGMENTS

THIS COOKBOOK would not be, were it not for the talent, hard work, and enthusiasm of the following people. I want to recognize them and offer my warmest thanks.

I deeply appreciate Sandra Day, who worked as chief editor. Her kindness and patience are remarkable. We couldn't have done it without you, Sandra.

My daughter Diane Broussard, who worked as junior editor, has earned my respect and gratitude for organizing and writing this book. Her dedication to detail and craftsmanship with the written word are superb.

My daughter Annette Oncale worked on the nutritional values and breakdown for every recipe. She also helped me test and retest countless recipes.

My daughter Toni Traylor also helped with the testing of recipes and kept my kitchen organized.

Howard "Poonie" Thomas is chief custodian at our restaurant. I know at times it was hard, but whenever I needed something cleaned in a hurry, Poonie came through.

I am grateful to the entire staff at Prudhomme's Cajun Cafe for their patience and support, especially my husband, Shelton.

We owe a huge debt of gratitude to Ann Bramson, Harriet Bell, Valerie Cimino, Laurie Orseck and Sarah Rutta at William Morrow for their enthusiasm and support.

INTRODUCTION

I WAS BORN the youngest girl in a family of thirteen children—ten brothers and two sisters. My family worked the land in South Louisiana as sharecroppers, farming on borrowed land and paying the landlord a third of our profits from the cotton and sweet-potato crops. We grew our own vegetables and raised our own animals for food. My mother was a fabulous cook, and I learned most of what I know about cooking from watching her prepare meal after meal for our family.

It wasn't long before I quit watching and started helping my mother in the kitchen. By the time I was twelve, I was preparing entire meals for the family. In those days if I decided to make smothered chicken, potato salad and a variety of vegetables for dinner, I would go out to the yard, select the lucky bird, kill it, clean it and then cook it. Then it was off to the barn to gather eggs, to the cellar to collect potatoes and to the garden to hand-pick vegetables. I usually had less than two hours to get our midday meal on the table. When Mama, Papa and my brothers and helpers came in from the fields, they were hungry and didn't want to wait! Everyone enjoyed my cooking (I never heard any complaints!), and I enjoyed it, too. I could eat as much as I wanted and never worry about gaining weight. But time has a way of changing things.

I was married at the age of fifteen and, as the years went by, became the mother of five children—two sons and three daughters. Once again the kitchen became the center of activity in my life. After my children were in school, I went to work to help support our family. But cooking still played a big part in my life. I loved cooking so much that I never thought of getting meals on the table as a chore. I looked forward to helping friends and family prepare for weddings, showers, family reunions and other special events.

My children grew up, got married and started families of their own, but we remained close, and Sundays, in particular, were special. I would cook a large meal for all my children, their spouses and my grandkids, and everyone would gather around the table to enjoy good food and conversation.

With no children to run around after and less work to keep me occupied, I gained twenty-four pounds. I felt uneasy and self-conscious about my appearance, and I knew my cooking and eating habits were affecting my health. I also knew, in the back of my mind, that I should do something about it. What really forced me to lose weight was a visit to my doctor, who told me my gallbladder had to be removed and recommended that I lose as much excess weight as possible before surgery.

After years of cooking and eating rich Cajun foods made with high-calorie and high-fat ingredients, I had to rethink everything I knew about preparing my favorite foods. I did not "diet." I began experimenting with ingredients that were lower in calories, fat and sodium. I substituted cottage cheese for cream, evaporated skim milk for whole milk, nonstick vegetable cooking spray for butter and so on. In three months I lost twenty-four pounds. And I've made my low-calorie Cajun cooking part of my everyday eating plan.

But life has its ups and downs. I was in the process of a divorce and feeling very depressed. I knew I needed a change of scene to keep my mind off my troubles and help me get back on my feet. My youngest brother, Paul, was planning to open a new business above his restaurant in New Orleans. He offered me a job as manager, and I stayed for one very happy year, doing what I love best, working with the public and cooking.

But pleas from a pregnant daughter convinced me to come home. Well, I love my children and my grandchildren, but I also love working, so I decided to take the bull by the horns and opened my own restaurant with the help and encouragement of my children, brother Paul and my wonderful new husband.

I opened my restaurant in a small building in historic Washington, Louisiana, which we outgrew in just two short years. I purchased and renovated a beautiful old Cajun house built in the 1880s, and from then on business really took off. The news spread quickly about the delicious food being served at Prudhomme's Cajun Cafe.

Sometimes while I was sitting at a back table in the restaurant having lunch, customers would ask, "What's that you're eating? I didn't see that on the menu, but it sure looks good."
I would answer, "It's a good unleaded meal."
"What's an unleaded meal?"
"It's something I prepare especially for myself that is low in calories and fat."
"When will it be on the menu?" everyone always asked.
It wasn't without objections from the kitchen, but I decided to include a few of these dishes on our daily menu. The demand for the recipes became so overwhelming that I decided to write this cookbook to share the healthy, flavorful, low-calorie food that we now serve in addition to our regular menu at Prudhomme's Cajun Cafe.

I hope you will visit our restaurant in Carencro, Louisiana. It is truly a family affair. When you enter our restaurant, you'll be greeted by my husband, Shelton, who is cashier and host. The person taking your order will most likely be one of my three

daughters, Annette, Diane or Toni; our granddaughters, Stacie and Liz; or Stacie's husband, Chris. And on it goes into the kitchen, where you'll find my son, Sonny; and two sons-in-law, Ike Broussard (Diane's husband), and Chris Oncale (Annette's husband); grandson Al Lanclos (Diane's son); and Henry Gillett, prepping and cooking. (Henry's been with us for some time, so he's like family!)

One last note: Each recipe is followed by calorie, fat, cholesterol and sodium information that has been analyzed by computer, based on N-Squared Computing Analytic Software, Nutritionist III. All nutrient breakdowns are listed per serving. All meats, fish and poultry are trimmed of fat (poultry is skinned). When a marinade is part of the recipe, only the amount used (not discarded) is calculated.

It is my fondest wish that with this book you will enjoy my favorite Cajun dishes prepared in healthy, yet delicious, ways and that you will receive the same benefits from this new way of cooking that I have.

C'est bon!

Enola Prudhomme

NOTES FROM OUR KITCHEN

ALLIGATOR GARFISH
In South Louisiana, this fish is commonly know as alligator-gar. With its long pointed head and very sharp teeth, it resembles the alligators found in local swamps. If garfish is not available, use any firm white-fleshed fish such as snapper, sea bass or trout.

BISQUE
A thick, rich Cajun soup usually made with crawfish, shrimp or crabmeat.

BREAD CRUMBS
The bread crumbs used in my book are homemade from bread (40 calories per slice) that has been toasted and made into bread crumbs in the blender or food processor.

BROWNING AND SEASONING SAUCE
A bottled, dark-brown liquid made from caramelized sugar, used to darken sauces and gravies.

CORNMEAL
We are so serious about our cornmeal that we use only freshly ground, yellow cornmeal, which is widely available in South Louisiana. Stone-ground cornmeal is available in supermarkets everywhere.

COTTAGE CHEESE
Many of the recipes in this book call for low-fat cottage cheese blended until smooth before using. Always keep some handy in your refrigerator.

CRABFINGERS
Also called fancy crab claws, these are cooked crab claws with the crabmeat intact but the shell has been removed except for one on the pincer of each claw. To eat them, hold the claw by the pincer with the shell and bite down, pulling the meat off the tendon with your teeth. Crabfingers can be found in the freezer section of your supermarket.

CRABMEAT
Fresh lump crabmeat is the only seafood I use that is precooked. It is readily available in supermarkets and seafood stores, usually in one-pound plastic containers. Before using crabmeat in any recipe, be sure to pick through it to remove any stray pieces of shell or tendon.

CRAWFISH
Crawfish are plentiful throughout Louisiana, and sometimes you can find them in your local markets, but if you can't find crawfish, substitute shrimp.

CREOLE MUSTARD
A specialty of Louisiana's German Creoles made from vinegar-marinated brown mustard seeds with a hint of horseradish. This hot, spicy mustard is available in the gourmet section of most supermarkets.

CROWDER PEA
A dried pea that is tan in color and resembles the black-eyed pea.

DRIED SALAD HERBS
A blend of dried herbs readily available in the spice section, it can be used on salads, poultry, meat or fish.

ETOUFFEE
Literally means "smothered," but in Cajun cooking it means covering food (seafood, vegetables or chicken) with a sauce.

FIELD PEA
A fresh garden pea popular in South Louisiana. It looks like miniature black-eyed pea. Black-eyed peas can be substituted.

FISH
Always use fresh fish, never frozen. If I've suggested a particular variety of fish that is not available in your area, feel free to substitute whatever fish is fresh in the market.

FRICASSÉE
A thick stew made from a brown roux for flavor and texture.

GREEN ONIONS
Cajuns prefer the term *green onions* to *scallions*, and we use plenty of them in our cooking. We grow them year-round in our backyards so we always have plenty on hand.

GRILLADES
Grillades are small pieces of boneless pork or beef that have been marinated overnight, then cooked in a sauce.

GUMBO
The famous Cajun soup. The basis of any gumbo is a dark roux that is traditionally made with flour and oil. The gumbos in my book are made from a roux with flour, but no oil. (See roux flour)

GUMBO FILÉ (FILÉ POWDER)
Finely ground sassafras leaves that is used for flavoring or as a thickener in gumbos and other Cajun dishes.

JAMBALAYA
A Cajun dish made with any meat or seafood, lots of seasonings and cooked rice. A great way to use leftover bits and pieces of ham, pork, sausage, chicken, etc.

MAQUE CHOUX
A sweet, yet highly seasoned corn dish. When I was a child, my Mama made maque choux with fresh-picked corn. It can also be made with chicken, crawfish or shrimp. Crawfish maque choux is one of our most popular dishes at Prudhomme's Cajun Cafe.

MARGARINE
Only reduced-calorie margarine is used in my recipes because it is lower in fat and calories than butter.

MILK
Most of our recipes call for canned, evaporated skim milk. A few recipes use regular skim milk, but never whole milk.

MIRLITON
This gourdlike fruit is about the size and shape of a very large pear and is also known as the chayote or vegetable pear. In South Louisiana, however, it is better known as the mirliton. Look for small, firm and unblemished fruit.

NONSTICK VEGETABLE COOKING SPRAY
I use cooking spray for oiling skillets, casseroles, sautéing, etc. Cooking spray contains fewer than 2½ calories per serving. In some recipes, I recommend using butter-flavored nonstick vegetable cooking spray.

OKRA
Okra can be boiled, pickled or steamed. Okra varies in size from 1 to 8 inches in length, but the smaller the pods, the more tender they are. When a recipe calls for whole okra, leave a portion of the stem attached. When boiling okra, use pods 1 to 3 inches long. While nothing beats the taste of fresh okra, frozen okra will do.

ONIONS
I can't imagine cooking without onions. I use a combination of fresh and dehydrated onions in my recipes. I find the dehydrated onions cut the cooking time in some of the recipes.

OYSTERS
If you are lucky enough to live near oyster beds that are harvested, use them. If you buy already-shucked oysters in their liquor, don't throw the liquor away; use it to make seafood stock—it is too delicious to waste.

PECAN MEAL
Pecan meal is simply pecans that have been very finely ground in a food processor or blender to a flourlike consistency. It can be found in most supermarkets in the South, or you can make your own, but be careful not to overprocess or you will end up with pecan butter.

PEPPERS
Black (freshly ground), red (ground), white (ground) and red and green bell peppers (fresh) are staples in my kitchen, and almost every recipe in this book uses them in one combination or another.

QUICK-MIXING FLOUR
A unique flour that makes lighter cuisine as simple as it is delicious. This flour is made by forming high-quality flour into "crystals" that mix instantly.

RABBIT
Use fresh domestic rabbit when possible. Dishes made with rabbit are growing in popularity because rabbit is low in calories and fat.

RICE
I use converted rice in all my recipes because it cooks faster and fluffier than regular rice.

ROUX FLOUR
Traditionally, a roux, the basis of many Cajun dishes, is made from slowly heating flour and oil, but who needs all those extra calories? I've developed a roux that contains only flour—no oil! By simply browning the flour, you can achieve the same flavor as a traditional roux. Once made, roux flour will keep for several months if stored in a tightly covered container.

SALT-FREE CHICKEN BOUILLON GRANULES
You can find these in most supermarkets. Mix with water to use as stock in the recipes if homemade stock is not available.

SHRIMP
While fresh-from-the-Gulf shrimp are always available in South Louisiana, any of these recipes can be prepared with shrimp found in your local market.

STOCK
Whether chicken or seafood, we make our own homemade stock at the restaurant. Stock adds a rich, hearty flavor to almost any dish. It is simple to make, freezes well and you can always double the recipe if you want to keep some on hand.

TASSO
Tasso is a highly seasoned smoked meat, used mainly for flavoring. I use turkey breast to make the tasso in my low-calorie recipes. I use very little salt, but the flavor is fantastic.

TURKEY
Many of the recipes use turkey in place of beef and even chicken. Turkey is low in calories and fat, and offers endless possibilities.

TURKEY SAUSAGE
I love the flavor of smoked pork sausage, but having a history of intestinal problems, I can't tolerate the fat. One day, I was experimenting with different ways of using fresh turkey breast when I decided to make my own smoked turkey sausage. It's delicious and not greasy. You can also buy turkey sausage in the supermarket and smoke it yourself at home.

VEGETABLES
Whenever possible, use fresh vegetables that are in season. There are times you may have to use frozen vegetables, but when properly prepared, frozen okra, corn, peas and spinach can be just as delicious as fresh. Many of the vegetable recipes reflect the Cajun way of cooking vegetables—long, slow cooking. If you prefer your vegetables less well done, adjust the cooking times according to taste.

STOCKS, GUMBOS

AND SOUPS

ROUX FLOUR

MAKES 4 CUPS

TRADITIONALLY a roux is made from flour *and* fat, but who can afford all those extra calories? A roux lends taste and texture to many Cajun dishes, so I've developed a roux, made by simply browning the flour, that adds the same flavor as fat-based roux.

This recipe is used in other recipes throughout the book. It's not hard to make, but like a traditional roux, it does require your full attention—so no phone calls or interruptions when making it!

If stored in a tightly covered container, roux flour will keep for 2 to 3 months.

4 cups all-purpose flour

Place the flour in a large skillet over high heat; with a wire whisk stir constantly for 25 minutes, or until the flour turns the color of light brown sugar. If the flour begins to darken too fast, remove the skillet from the heat and stir to allow flour to cool and color evenly before putting it back on a lower heat setting.

Remove from the heat and continue stirring until the flour is completely cooled. Sift the flour into a container, and store, covered, until needed.

PER CUP	KCAL	FATgm	CHOLmg	SODmg
	340	1	0	0

SEAFOOD STOCK

2 to 3 *pounds rinsed shrimp heads and/or shells, crawfish heads and/or crab shells, or rinsed fish carcasses (heads and gills removed), or any combination of these*
4 *quarts water*

In a large stockpot combine the ingredients and bring to a boil. Reduce the heat, cover, and simmer for 3 to 4 hours, or until the liquid is reduced by half. Remove from the heat and strain through a sieve. Allow the stock to cool slightly, then refrigerate or freeze in batches until needed.

Nutritional information not available.

CHICKEN STOCK

MAKES ABOUT 4 QUARTS

5½ pounds meaty chicken
bones or chicken
wings and backs
2 medium onions,
unpeeled and
quartered
8 quarts water
2 medium carrots, cut in
half lengthwise

1 bunch green onions
(white part only)
1 bunch fresh parsley
stems
10 black peppercorns
2 bay leaves

Preheat the oven to 400°F.

Place the chicken bones or wings and backs and the onions in a 5-quart Dutch oven. Bake for 45 minutes, or until browned. Remove the pot from the oven and add one-half the water, stirring and scraping the bottom of the pot until all the brown bits are loosened.

Transfer everything to a large stockpot and place over high heat. Add the remaining quarts of water and all the rest of the ingredients and bring to a boil.

Reduce the heat to medium and simmer, uncovered, for 20 minutes. Cover, reduce the heat and simmer for 2 to 3 hours, or until the liquid has been reduced by half. Remove the stock from the heat and strain through a sieve, discarding all the remains. Allow the stock to cool slightly, then refrigerate overnight.

The next day, using a spoon, skim all the congealed fat from the top of the stock before using. Refrigerate or freeze the stock in covered containers until needed.

Nutritional information not available.

CHICKEN AND TURKEY SAUSAGE GUMBO

MAKES 6 MAIN-COURSE SERVINGS

One 1½-to-2-pound
  chicken, cut into
  serving-size pieces,
  skin and fat removed
9 cups water
½ pound Smoked Turkey
  Sausage (page 110),
  cut into bite-size
  pieces
2 cups finely chopped
  onions
½ cup finely chopped
  green bell pepper
½ cup finely chopped
  celery

2⅓ cups Roux Flour
  (page 18)
1½ teaspoons salt
1 teaspoon ground red
  pepper
1 bay leaf
½ cup finely chopped
  green onions
2 tablespoons very finely
  chopped fresh
  parsley

Remove the skin, fat and wings from the chicken pieces and discard. Spray the inside of a large skillet with nonstick vegetable cooking spray and place over high heat. Add the chicken and cook for 10 minutes, or until brown, turning often. Remove the skillet from the heat and transfer the chicken to a plate. Add 1 cup of the water to the skillet, scraping the bottom with a wooden spoon to loosen the brown bits; return the chicken to the skillet and set aside.

Place the remaining 8 cups water in a 5-quart Dutch oven over high heat and bring to a boil. Add the chicken and pan juices along with the remaining ingredients except for the green onions and parsley. Cook, uncovered, for 25 minutes, stirring occasionally. Stir in the green onions and parsley and cook for 5 more minutes. Remove the bay leaf before serving in bowls.

PER SERVING	KCAL	FATgm	CHOLmg	SODmg
	405	9	5	618

OKRA, CHICKEN AND SAUSAGE GUMBO

MAKES 6 SERVINGS

CHICKEN AND SAUSAGE gumbo is a favorite in Cajun country. Adding okra gives gumbo a special flavor and acts as a natural thickener.

1 *tablespoon reduced-calorie margarine*
Two *10-ounce packages frozen cut okra, thawed*
1 *cup finely chopped onions*
2 *tablespoons tomato paste*
5 *cups water*
½ *pound Smoked Turkey Sausage (page 110), cut into bite-size pieces*
2 *medium tomatoes, peeled, seeded and chopped (about 1 cup)*

2 *tablespoons Roux Flour (page 18)*
½ *teaspoon salt*
½ *teaspoon ground white pepper*
½ *teaspoon ground red pepper*
1 *bay leaf*
2 *chicken breast halves (about 5 ounces each), boned, skinned and cut into ½-inch strips*
1 *tablespoon salt-free chicken bouillon granules*

Melt the margarine in a medium skillet over high heat. Add the okra and cook for 10 minutes, or until the okra is no longer slimy, stirring constantly and scraping the bottom of the skillet with a wooden spoon. (If the okra starts to stick, remove the skillet from the heat and spray with nonstick vegetable cooking spray; return to the heat.) Reduce the heat to low and add the onions and tomato paste; cook, stirring for 5 minutes. Remove from the heat and set aside.

In a 4-quart Dutch oven over high heat, add 4 cups of water, the cooked okra, the sausage, tomatoes, roux flour, salt, white and red peppers and bay leaf. Cook, uncovered, for 15 minutes, stirring occasionally.

Spray the inside of a medium skillet with nonstick vegetable cooking spray and place over high heat. Add the chicken strips and sauté for 8 minutes, or until brown. Dissolve the bouillon in remaining 1 cup of water and add to the skillet, stirring well. Transfer the chicken and pan juices to the Dutch oven. Cook, covered, for an additional 15 minutes, stirring occasionally. Remove the bay leaf before serving over hot rice.

PER SERVING	KCAL	FATgm	CHOLmg	SODmg
	205	4	73	263

RABBIT AND TURKEY SAUSAGE GUMBO

MAKES 6 SERVINGS

1 tablespoon vegetable
   oil
1 pound boned rabbit
   meat
½ pound Smoked Turkey
   Sausage (page 110),
   cut into
   2-inch pieces
1 cup finely chopped
   onions
½ cup finely chopped
   celery
2 quarts Chicken Stock
   (page 20) or water
½ cup Roux Flour
   (page 18)

½ teaspoon salt
½ teaspoon ground white
   pepper
½ teaspoon ground red
   pepper
1 bay leaf
½ cup finely chopped
   green onions
2 tablespoons very finely
   chopped fresh
   parsley
1½ cups hot cooked rice

In a large pot over high heat, heat the oil until very hot. Add the rabbit and sausage and cook for 10 minutes, or until brown, stirring constantly. Add the onions and celery; cook, stirring constantly for 10 minutes. Add the stock and cook, uncovered, for 20 minutes, stirring often.

Stir in the roux flour, salt, white and red peppers, and bay leaf and continue cooking for 20 minutes, stirring occasionally. Add the green onions and parsley. Cover and cook for 5 minutes. Remove the pot from the heat and let stand for 5 minutes. Remove the bay leaf and serve over rice.

PER SERVING	KCAL	FATgm	CHOLmg	SODmg
	331	4	32	237

SHRIMP AND OKRA GUMBO

MAKES 3 MAIN-COURSE SERVINGS

Two 10-ounce packages
  frozen cut okra, thawed
  (4 cups)
3 *cups Seafood Stock*
  (page 19) or water
1 *medium tomato,*
  peeled, seeded and
  chopped (about ½
  cup)
1 *cup finely chopped*
  onions
½ *pound medium shrimp,*
  peeled and deveined
2 *tablespoons Roux Flour*
  (see page 18)

2 *teaspoons paprika*
1 *teaspoon salt*
½ *teaspoon ground white*
  pepper
½ *teaspoon ground*
  oregano
½ *teaspoon ground red*
  pepper
½ *teaspoon hot pepper*
  sauce
1 *bay leaf*
¼ *cup finely chopped*
  green onions
1 *cup hot cooked rice*

Spray the inside of a large saucepan with nonstick vegetable cooking spray and place over high heat. Add the okra and cook for 15 minutes, stirring constantly and scraping the bottom of the saucepan with a wooden spoon. (If okra starts to stick, remove the pan from the heat and spray again; return to heat.)

Reduce the heat to medium and stir in all the remaining ingredients except for the green onions and rice. Cover and cook for 25 minutes, stirring occasionally. Remove from the heat and stir in the green onions. Remove the bay leaf. Let stand for 10 minutes before serving. Serve over hot rice.

PER SERVING	KCAL	FATgm	CHOLmg	SODmg
	171	2	148	585

SHRIMP AND TURKEY SAUSAGE GUMBO

MAKES 5 MAIN-COURSE SERVINGS

1 *tablespoon vegetable oil*

2 *cups finely chopped onions*

⅓ *cup finely chopped celery*

7 *cups Seafood Stock (page 19) or water*

½ *pound Smoked Turkey Sausage (page 110), cut into 2-inch pieces*

½ *cup Roux Flour (page 18)*

½ *pound medium shrimp, peeled and deveined*

⅓ *cup finely chopped green onions*

2 *tablespoons finely chopped fresh parsley*

2½ *cups hot cooked rice*

In a heavy 5-quart saucepan over high heat, heat the oil until very hot. Add the onions and celery; sauté, stirring for 10 minutes. Add the stock, sausage and roux flour and cook for 20 minutes, stirring occasionally. Add the shrimp, green onions and parsley; cook for 15 minutes. Serve over hot rice.

PER SERVING	KCAL	FATgm	CHOLmg	SODmg
	173	4	82	95

SEAFOOD GUMBO

MAKES 4 MAIN-COURSE SERVINGS

2 quarts water
1¼ cups Roux Flour
    (page 18)
1½ cups finely chopped
    onions
½ cup finely chopped
    celery
½ pound cocktail
    crabfingers
½ pound medium shrimp,
    peeled and deveined

1 cup shucked oysters
1 teaspoon ground red
    pepper
1 teaspoon freshly
    ground black pepper
½ cup finely chopped
    green onions
1 tablespoon very finely
    chopped fresh
    parsley
2 cups hot cooked rice

In a large pot over high heat, bring the water to a boil. Stir in the roux flour, onions and celery. Reduce the heat to medium and simmer for 45 minutes, stirring often.

Stir in the crabfingers, shrimp, oysters and red and black peppers; simmer for 15 minutes. Add the green onions and parsley, and cook for an additional 5 minutes. Let stand for 20 minutes before serving. Serve over hot rice.

PER SERVING	KCAL	FATgm	CHOLmg	SODmg
	390	4	181	488

CRABMEAT BISQUE

MAKES 6 SERVINGS

A rich Cajun soup that can also be made with crawfish or shrimp.

One-half 10-ounce package frozen tiny green peas, thawed
1 *cup Seafood Stock (page 19) or water*
One 8-ounce can condensed tomato soup
2 *teaspoons dehydrated onion*
1 *cup evaporated skim milk*
2 *cups skim milk*

¼ *teaspoon salt*
¼ *teaspoon ground white pepper*
¼ *teaspoon garlic powder*
¼ *teaspoon ground oregano*
¼ *teaspoon ground red pepper*
1 *pound fresh lump crabmeat, picked over*

Place the peas in a food processor or blender container and process until smooth. In a large saucepan over medium heat, combine the pureed peas, stock and tomato soup. Cook for 15 minutes, stirring often. Add the onion, evaporated skim milk and seasonings. Reduce the heat and simmer for 15 minutes, stirring often. Add the crabmeat; simmer for 3 minutes and serve hot.

PER SERVING	KCAL	FATgm	CHOLmg	SODmg
	70	2	139	158

CORN SOUP CAJUN-STYLE

MAKES 3 SERVINGS

1 tablespoon quick-
   mixing flour
½ cup water
1 tablespoon margarine
3 cups fresh corn, cut off
   the cob (about 6 ears)
½ cup finely chopped
   onions
2 medium tomatoes,
   peeled, seeded and
   chopped (about 1 cup)

2 cups skim milk
1 cup evaporated skim
   milk
¼ teaspoon salt
¼ teaspoon ground white
   pepper
⅛ teaspoon ground red
   pepper
3 tablespoons finely
   chopped green onions

In a small bowl, dissolve the flour in the water; set aside. In a medium saucepan over medium heat melt the margarine. Add the corn, onion and tomatoes; cook for 15 minutes, stirring constantly.

Add the skim milk and simmer for an additional 15 minutes. Add the evaporated skim milk, dissolved flour, salt, and the white and red peppers. Reduce the heat and simmer for 15 minutes, stirring often. Add the green onions, simmer for 5 minutes and serve hot.

PER SERVING	KCAL	FATgm	CHOLmg	SODmg
	343	5	10	406

CORN CHOWDER

MAKES 8 1-CUP SERVINGS OR 4 MAIN-COURSE SERVINGS

WHEN MY CAJUN ancestors emigrated from Nova Scotia to South Louisiana, they learned how to cook corn from the Indians living in the Louisiana bayou. Corn became a very important part of our cuisine, and it still is today.

2 *slices lean bacon, cut into 1-inch pieces*
1½ *cups finely chopped onions*
½ *cup finely chopped green bell pepper*
½ *cup finely chopped celery*
2 *medium potatoes, peeled and cut into ½-inch cubes*
1 *tablespoon salt-free chicken bouillon granules*
2½ *cups water*

One 10-ounce package frozen whole-kernel corn, thawed
1 *teaspoon salt*
½ *teaspoon granulated garlic*
¼ *teaspoon ground red pepper*
¼ *teaspoon ground oregano*
2½ *cups evaporated skim milk*
⅓ *cup finely chopped green onions*

In a heavy 5-quart saucepan over high heat, fry the bacon until crisp. Remove the bacon and drain on paper towels, then crumble. Drain bacon grease, reserving *1 tablespoon* in the same saucepan.

Add the onions, bell pepper, celery, and potatoes to the saucepan and sauté over medium heat for 10 minutes. Dissolve the bouillon in the water and add to the saucepan along with the corn, salt, garlic, red pepper and oregano; bring to a boil.

Reduce the heat and simmer, covered, for 15 minutes, or until the potatoes are tender, stirring occasionally.

Meanwhile, in a small saucepan over high heat, heat the milk until very hot, but do not boil. Remove the milk from the heat and add to the corn mixture, stirring well. Reduce the heat and simmer, covered, for 10 minutes. Ladle the hot soup into serving bowls. Garnish with the green onions and serve.

PER CUP	KCAL	FATgm	CHOLmg	SODmg
	153	2	6	537

GULF SNAPPER SOUP

MAKES 4 MAIN-COURSE SERVINGS

MY SON, Sonny, won an award with this dish in the Seafood Challenge Contest.

1 *cup finely chopped onions*
1 *clove garlic, minced*
5 *cups Seafood Stock (page 19) or water*
1 *medium tomato, peeled, seeded and chopped (about ½ cup)*
⅓ *cup tomato sauce*
¼ *teaspoon hot pepper sauce*
½ *teaspoon salt*
1 *teaspoon ground oregano*

¼ *teaspoon ground thyme*
¼ *teaspoon ground red pepper*
1 *tablespoon Roux Flour (page 18)*
1 *bay leaf*
1 *pound red snapper fillets, cut into 1-inch pieces; or use any mild, white-fleshed fish*

Spray the inside of a 6-quart pot with nonstick vegetable cooking spray and place over medium heat. Add the onions and garlic and cook for 3 minutes, stirring constantly. Add all of the remaining ingredients except the fish. Reduce the heat and simmer, uncovered, for 20 minutes. Add the fish, cover and simmer for 8 to 10 minutes, until the fish flakes with a fork. Remove the bay leaf before serving.

PER SERVING	KCAL	FATgm	CHOLmg	SODmg
	149	1.8	41	335

TURKEY AND BARLEY SOUP

MAKES 4 SERVINGS

6 *cups water*
¼ *cup barley*
1 *cup chopped onions*
½ *cup chopped celery*
1 *tablespoon salt-free chicken bouillon granules*
½ *pound turkey breast, boned, skinned and cut into bite-size pieces*

1 *teaspoon sour-cream-and-butter-flavored sprinkles*
½ *teaspoon salt-free lemon-pepper seasoning*

In a large saucepan over high heat, bring the water to a boil. Add the barley, reduce the heat and simmer for 15 minutes, stirring occasionally. Add the onions, celery and bouillon granules and continue cooking for 20 minutes. Add the remaining ingredients and cook for 20 minutes longer, until the barley and turkey are tender.

PER SERVING	KCAL	FATgm	CHOLmg	SODmg
	87	0.45	0	379

SPICY COUNTRY VEGETABLE SOUP

MAKES 6 MAIN-COURSE SERVINGS

THIS SOUP is delicious and easy to prepare. It's especially good on cold winter nights, and can be served as a first course or a main meal. Leftovers can be frozen, but if you have children like mine, there's never any left over!

6 *cups Chicken Stock (page 20) or water*
3 *medium tomatoes, peeled and chopped (about 1½ cups)*
2 *medium carrots, thinly sliced (1 cup)*
1 *medium onion, thinly sliced*
½ *medium green bell pepper, thinly sliced*
One *10-ounce package frozen cut green beans*

One *6-ounce can tomato paste*
2 *cups fresh broccoli florets*
2 *cups fresh cauliflowerets*
1 *cup frozen whole-kernel corn*
1 *teaspoon salt*
½ *teaspoon ground white pepper*
½ *teaspoon hot pepper sauce (optional)*

In a 6-quart pot, combine all the ingredients and place over medium heat. Cover and cook for 45 minutes, stirring occasionally.

PER SERVING	KCAL	FATgm	CHOLmg	SODmg
	87	0.45	0	378

WHITE BEAN SOUP

MAKES 4 MAIN-COURSE SERVINGS

1 *pound dry white beans*
7 *cups hot water*
1 *cup chopped onions*
¼ *cup chopped green bell pepper*
¼ *cup chopped celery*
2 *cloves garlic, minced*
½ *teaspoon salt*
½ *teaspoon ground marjoram*

½ *teaspoon dried dillweed*
¼ *teaspoon ground red pepper*
⅛ *teaspoon ground black pepper*
¼ *cup chopped green onions*

Place the beans in a large pot and add enough water to cover; let them soak for 8 hours or overnight. Drain the beans.

In the same pot, combine the beans, hot water and the remaining ingredients, except for the green onions, and place over medium heat. Simmer, covered, for 1 hour, or until the beans are tender, stirring occasionally. Remove from the heat and stir in the green onions; let the soup stand for 10 minutes before serving.

PER SERVING	KCAL	FATgm	CHOLmg	SODmg
	181	0.92	0	269

"CREAM" OF MUSHROOM SOUP

MAKES 2 SERVINGS

THIS CAN BE USED in recipes in place of canned cream of mushroom soup.

1 *cup cold skim milk*
1 *tablespoon quick-*
   mixing flour
1 *tablespoon reduced-*
   calorie margarine
½ *teaspoon ground white*
   pepper

⅛ *teaspoon ground red*
   pepper
¼ *teaspoon salt*
1 *small onion, sliced*
1 *pound finely chopped*
   fresh mushrooms

In a large saucepan over low heat, combine the milk, flour, margarine, white and red peppers, salt and onion; cook, stirring constantly for 10 minutes, or until the mixture begins to thicken. Remove from the heat and pour the mixture through a strainer. Discard the onion. Return the strained soup to the saucepan; add the mushrooms and cook over medium heat for 5 minutes, stirring often.

PER SERVING	KCAL	FATgm	CHOLmg	SODmg
	197	4	5	381

CHICKEN AND PASTA SOUP

MAKES 6 SERVINGS

MY GRANDAUGHTER Leigh was in the restaurant when I made this dish. She ate a spoonful and said, "Maw Maw, this is good!"

Note: Rotini is a corkscrew-shaped pasta that is made with vegetables such as spinach, carrots or beets to give it color.

One 2-to-2½-pound chicken, skin and fat removed
Water
¾ cup chopped green bell pepper
½ cup chopped celery
½ teaspoon salt
½ teaspoon salt-free lemon-pepper seasoning

⅛ teaspoon ground white pepper
⅛ teaspoon ground red pepper
1 bay leaf
1 cup uncooked three-color vegetable rotini
1 cup finely chopped red bell pepper
⅓ cup finely chopped green onions

Place the chicken in a 6-quart pot and cover with water. Bring to a boil; reduce the heat and simmer for 1 hour, or until tender. Remove the chicken from the stock and allow to sit until cool enough to handle. Remove the meat from the bones and cut into bite-size pieces. Discard the bones. Return the chicken meat to the stock and add the green bell pepper, celery, salt, lemon-pepper seasoning, white and red peppers and bay leaf. Simmer for 20 minutes, stirring often. Remove the bay leaf. Add the rotini and cook for an additional 10 minutes. Add the red bell pepper and green onions and cook for 2 minutes. Serve hot.

PER SERVING	KCAL	FATgm	CHOLmg	SODmg
	244	7	86	414

BROCCOLI SOUP

MAKES 3 SERVINGS

4 *cups fresh broccoli florets and coarsely chopped stems*
Water
One 10½-ounce can reduced-calorie cream of mushroom soup
2 *tablespoons dehydrated onion*

¼ *teaspoon dehydrated bell pepper*
1 *cup evaporated skim milk*
1 *tablespoon salt-free chicken bouillon granules*
½ *cup shredded reduced-fat Cheddar cheese*

Place the broccoli in a medium saucepan and cover with water; place over high heat and bring to a boil. Cook for 10 to 15 minutes, or until tender; drain, reserving the cooking liquid.

Place the cooked broccoli in a food processor and process carefully until finely chopped but not pureed; set aside. In the saucepan with the reserved liquid combine the mushroom soup, onion, bell pepper and chopped broccoli. Place over medium heat and simmer, covered, for 15 minutes, stirring often.

Meanwhile, in a small saucepan, combine the milk and bouillon; heat until very hot, but do not boil. Cook, stirring, for 5 minutes, then remove from the heat and add to the broccoli mixture. Stir in the cheese and cook for 1 minute. Serve hot.

PER SERVING	KCAL	FATgm	CHOLmg	SODmg
	179	4.5	13	614

SALADS AND SALAD DRESSINGS

SPICY CORN SALAD

MAKES 4 SERVINGS

THIS DISH can be served as a main meal or a side dish with meat or poultry.

One 10-ounce package frozen whole-kernel corn or 6 ears fresh corn, cut off the cob (about 2 cups)
1 *cup low-fat cottage cheese*
½ *cup finely chopped onions*
⅓ *cup finely chopped green bell pepper*
1 *teaspoon finely chopped pimiento*

1 *teaspoon finely chopped fresh parsley*
¼ *teaspoon salt*
⅛ *teaspoon ground white pepper*
⅛ *teaspoon ground black pepper*
1 *tablespoon balsamic vinegar*
1 *tablespoon reduced-calorie mayonnaise*

In a medium saucepan, cook the corn according to the directions on the package, omitting the salt and cooking for only 5 minutes. Place the cottage cheese in a blender and process until smooth. Reserve *1 tablespoon* of the pureed cottage cheese; refrigerate the remaining for another use.

Combine the corn, the pureed cottage cheese and all the remaining ingredients, stirring to mix well. Cover and refrigerate for 6 hours before serving.

PER SERVING	KCAL	FATgm	CHOLmg	SODmg
	80	1.2	1.4	141

CABBAGE AND CARROT SALAD

MAKES 4 SERVINGS

1 cup low-fat cottage cheese
1 medium apple, cut into ½-inch cubes
1 large carrot, shredded (about ½ cup)
½ small cabbage, shredded (about 3 cups)

⅓ cup raisins
1 tablespoon balsamic vinegar
1 tablespoon reduced-calorie mayonnaise
½ teaspoon ground black pepper
¼ teaspoon salt

In a blender, process the cottage cheese until smooth. Reserve ⅓ cup and refrigerate the rest for another use.

In a large bowl, combine the cottage cheese with the remaining ingredients and toss well. Chill for 1 hour before serving.

PER SERVING	KCAL	FATgm	CHOLmg	SODmg
	117	1.8	3.75	362

BROCCOLI AND CAULIFLOWER SALAD

MAKES 4 SERVINGS

1 *cup low-fat cottage cheese*
2 *cups fresh broccoli florets*
2 *cups fresh cauliflowerets*
½ *cup reduced-calorie mayonnaise*
2 *teaspoons sugar*

¼ *teaspoon salt*
½ *teaspoon ground white pepper*
½ *teaspoon ground black pepper*
½ *teaspoon dried dillweed*
½ *cup very finely chopped green onions*

In a blender, process the cottage cheese until smooth. Reserve ⅓ cup and refrigerate the rest for another use.

Place the broccoli and cauliflower in a large bowl. In a small bowl, combine the mayonnaise, sugar, salt, white and black peppers, dillweed and cottage cheese.

Pour the dressing over the vegetables, add the green onions and toss well. Chill well before serving.

PER SERVING	KCAL	FATgm	CHOLmg	SODmg
	128	8.5	11	218

HOT POTATO SALAD

MAKES 3 SERVINGS

2 *medium potatoes,*
  peeled and cut into
  1-inch cubes
1 *hard-cooked egg,*
  peeled and chopped
1 *small dill pickle, finely*
  chopped
1 *tablespoon very finely*
  chopped onions

2 *tablespoons reduced-*
  calorie mayonnaise
⅛ *teaspoon salt*
⅛ *teaspoon ground white*
  pepper
⅛ *teaspoon dry hot*
  mustard
⅛ *teaspoon ground black*
  pepper

Place the potatoes in a medium saucepan with enough water to cover and bring to a boil. Cook for 15 minutes, until the potatoes are tender; drain and set aside.

In a large bowl, combine the remaining ingredients; mix well. Add the potatoes, toss well and serve hot.

PER SERVING	KCAL	FATgm	CHOLmg	SODmg
	100	5	95	419

CREAMY COLE SLAW

MAKES 4 SERVINGS

A DELICIOUS side dish, light and creamy, yet filling.

1 *cup low-fat cottage cheese*
½ *small head cabbage, shredded (about 2 cups)*
⅓ *cup raisins*
1 *medium carrot, shredded (about ¼ cup)*

2 *tablespoons reduced-calorie mayonnaise*
¼ *teaspoon salt*
⅛ *teaspoon ground white pepper*

In a blender, process the cottage cheese until smooth. Reserve ½ cup and refrigerate the rest for another use.

In a large bowl, soak the cabbage in enough cold water to cover for 10 minutes, then drain well. Add the raisins, carrots and the pureed cottage cheese; toss well. Add the mayonnaise, salt and pepper, and stir until well mixed. Serve immediately on chili until ready to serve.

PER SERVING	KCAL	FATgm	CHOLmg	SODmg
	95	2.5	3.8	252

OLD-TIME CABBAGE SLAW

MAKES 4 SERVINGS

A DELICIOUS substitute for a green salad.

1 *small head cabbage, shredded (about 4 cups)*
3 *tablespoons apple cider vinegar*
¼ *teaspoon ground black pepper*

In a large bowl, soak the cabbage in enough cold water to cover for 5 minutes. Drain well. Add the remaining ingredients and toss until well mixed. Refrigerate for at least 1 hour before serving.

PER SERVING	KCAL	FATgm	CHOLmg	SODmg
	22	0.18	0	11

SEAFOOD SALAD

MAKES 4 SERVINGS

1 cup water
10 medium sea scallops
10 medium shrimp, peeled
 and deveined
6 large oysters, shucked
¼ cup finely chopped
 green onions
¼ teaspoon salt
⅛ teaspoon ground
 oregano
⅛ teaspoon ground black
 pepper
½ cup fresh lump
 crabmeat, picked
 over

16 large lettuce leaves
 (romaine or leaf)
2 cups coarsely chopped
 iceberg lettuce
2 cups coarsely chopped
 Boston lettuce
½ cup finely chopped
 celery
½ cup finely chopped
 green bell pepper

In a medium skillet, bring the water to a boil. Add the scallops, shrimp, oysters, green onions, salt, oregano and pepper and simmer, uncovered, for 3 minutes. Reduce the heat to medium; add the crabmeat and cook 1 minute longer. Drain the seafood in a sieve, reserving the liquid, and set the seafood aside to cool.

On 4 salad plates, arrange 4 overlapping lettuce leaves. In a large bowl, toss together the chopped lettuces, celery and bell pepper, and then mound on the lettuce leaves and top with the seafood. Spoon about 2 tablespoons of the reserved seafood liquid over each salad.

PER SERVING	KCAL	FATgm	CHOLmg	SODmg
	96	1.5	56	405

SHRIMP SALAD

MAKES 4 SERVINGS

1 *cup water*
20 *medium shrimp, peeled and deveined*
¼ *teaspoon salt*
¼ *teaspoon garlic powder*
¼ *teaspoon ground oregano*
¼ *teaspoon ground black pepper*
16 *large lettuce leaves (romaine or leaf)*
4 *cups chopped iceberg lettuce*
½ *cup finely chopped celery*
½ *cup finely chopped green bell pepper*
½ *cup finely chopped red bell pepper*
½ *cup finely chopped dill pickle*
½ *cup finely chopped onions*
3 *large pimiento-stuffed olives, chopped*
4 *medium tomatoes, quartered*

In a large skillet, bring the water to a boil. Add the shrimp, salt, garlic powder, oregano and pepper, then reduce the heat to medium. Simmer for 3 minutes, or until the shrimp turn pink, stirring often. Remove from the heat, drain the shrimp and set aside.

On each of 4 salad plates, arrange 4 overlapping lettuce leaves. In a bowl, toss together the chopped iceberg, celery, bell pepper, pickle, onions and olives. Divide equally and mound on the lettuce leaves. Top each with half of the cooked shrimp and 2 *tablespoons* of the cooking liquid from the shrimp. Garnish with the tomatoes and serve.

PER SERVING	KCAL	FATgm	CHOLmg	SODmg
	102	1.5	90	424

GRILLED CATFISH SALAD

MAKES 2 SERVINGS

THIS IS a perfect way to use leftover grilled catfish.

Two 5-ounce catfish fillets
⅛ teaspoon salt
⅛ teaspoon ground oregano
⅛ teaspoon ground black
 pepper
8 large lettuce leaves
 (romaine or leaf)
2 cups coarsely chopped
 lettuce

1 cup coarsely chopped
 fresh spinach
¼ cup chopped green
 onions
½ cup thinly sliced
 fresh mushrooms
½ cup shredded red
 cabbage
¼ cup finely chopped
 celery

Season the fish with the salt, oregano and pepper; place on hot grill and cook until fish flakes easily with a fork. Remove from the heat and set aside.

On each of 2 salad plates, arrange 4 overlapping lettuce leaves. In a large bowl, toss together the remaining ingredients and divide between the 2 plates. Cut the fish into bite-size pieces and arrange on top of the salads. If desired, serve with Jason's Dressing, but remember that that will add extra calories!

PER SERVING	KCAL	FATgm	CHOLmg	SODmg
	201	3.3	76	313

CREAMY BUTTERMILK DRESSING

MAKES 1¼ CUPS

1 *cup buttermilk*
3 *tablespoons plain low-fat yogurt*
2 *tablespoons finely chopped onions*
1 *teaspoon cornstarch*
1 *teaspoon lemon juice*

½ *teaspoon granulated garlic*
½ *teaspoon dried salad herbs*
¼ *teaspoon ground oregano*
⅛ *teaspoon salt*

Combine all the ingredients in a blender; blend on high speed for 10 seconds, or until smooth and creamy. Chill until ready to serve.

PER TABLESPOON	KCAL	FATgm	CHOLmg	SODmg
	8	0.1	0.6	28

GARLIC-DILL DRESSING

MAKES ABOUT 1 CUP

½ cup reduced-calorie
soft-style cream
cheese
¼ cup plain low-fat yogurt
¼ cup finely chopped
green onions

2 cloves garlic, minced
3 tablespoons finely
chopped dill pickle
2 teaspoons lemon juice
2 teaspoons low-sodium
Worcestershire sauce

In a blender, puree the cream cheese and yogurt together until smooth. Add the remaining ingredients and blend for 1 minute. Pour into a jar, cover and refrigerate until needed. Shake well before serving.

PER TABLESPOON	KCAL	FATgm	CHOLmg	SODmg
	21	1.3	0.21	7

JASON'S DRESSING

MAKES ABOUT 1½ CUPS

*J*MY GRANDSON JASON is thirteen years old and fast becoming a great little chef. He loves to cook and help in the kitchen. I often bring him along to help me with my cooking demos.

¼ *cup bottled chili sauce*	2 *teaspoons minced fresh*
½ *cup reduced-calorie*	*onion*
mayonnaise	½ *teaspoon low-sodium*
1 *tablespoon honey*	*Worcestershire sauce*

Combine all the ingredients in a small bowl and whisk until well mixed. Cover and refrigerate for at least 1 hour before serving.

PER TABLESPOON	KCAL	FATgm	CHOLmg	SODmg
	19	1.3	1.5	34

CREAMY HERB DRESSING

MAKES 2 CUPS

1 *cup buttermilk*
½ *cup plain low-fat yogurt*
2 *tablespoons reduced-*
   calorie mayonnaise
2 *tablespoons minced*
   fresh onion
2 *teaspoons minced fresh*
   garlic

1 *tablespoon balsamic*
   vinegar
1 *teaspoon lemon juice*
¼ *teaspoon dry mustard*
⅛ *teaspoon ground white*
   pepper

Combine all the ingredients in a food processor or blender and process until smooth. Store in a tightly covered jar in the refrigerator until needed.

PER SERVING	KCAL	FATgm	CHOLmg	SODmg
	8	0.37	0.81	11

VINAIGRETTE DRESSING

MAKES ABOUT 1 CUP

½ cup white vinegar
¼ cup water
3 tablespoons extra virgin
   olive oil

2 tablespoons red wine
   vinegar
1 tablespoon sugar
1 teaspoon Dijon mustard

Combine all the ingredients in a blender; blend at medium speed until smooth. Pour into a jar; cover and refrigerate until needed. Shake well before serving.

PER TABLESPOON	KCAL	FATgm	CHOLmg	SODmg
	15	1.2	0	4

GREEN ONION DRESSING

MAKES 2 CUPS

1½ cups chopped green
   onions
1 tablespoon chopped
   jalapeño peppers
1 cup buttermilk
½ cup plain low-fat
   yogurt

⅓ cup reduced-calorie
   soft-style cream
   cheese
1 teaspoon tarragon
   vinegar

Spray the inside of a medium skillet with nonstick vegetable cooking spray. Heat the skillet over high heat and add the green onions and jalapeños. Sauté for 2 minutes; remove from the heat and set aside.

When cool, combine the onion mixture with all the remaining ingredients in a blender; blend on high for 5 minutes, or until the mixture is smooth. Refrigerate in a covered jar until needed; shake well before serving.

PER TABLESPOON	KCAL	FATgm	CHOLmg	SODmg
	8	0.28	0.50	20

HERB DRESSING

MAKES 2 CUPS

1 *cup water*
2 *tablespoons red wine*
   vinegar
1 *tablespoon rice wine*
   vinegar

1 *teaspoon dried salad*
   herbs
1 *teaspoon onion powder*
½ *teaspoon garlic powder*
⅛ *teaspoon salt*

Combine all the ingredients in a covered jar and shake well. Store the dressing in the refrigerator for up to several weeks; shake well before using.

PER TABLESPOON	KCAL	FATgm	CHOLmg	SODmg
	0.52	0	0	8

COUNTRY DRESSING

MAKES 2 CUPS

WE OFTEN THINK of dressings being used only with salads, but this one goes well with broiled shrimp or other seafoods.

½ cup low-fat cottage cheese
½ cup plain low-fat yogurt
⅓ cup bottled low-sodium chili sauce
2 tablespoons prepared horseradish
1 tablespoon minced fresh onion
1 tablespoon very finely chopped fresh parsley
1 tablespoon balsamic vinegar
1 teaspoon low-sodium Worcestershire sauce

Combine all the ingredients in a blender; process until smooth. Store in a covered jar and refrigerate until needed. Shake well before using.

PER TABLESPOON	KCAL	FATgm	CHOLmg	SODmg
	7	1	0.38	30

SHELLFISH

STUFFED CRAB A LA AL

MAKES 2 SERVINGS

J TRY DOUBLING this recipe and freezing some for later use. Stored in an airtight container, this will freeze for 2 months. Decorative ceramic or aluminum crab shells can be found in housewares departments.

2 slices bread (40 calories per slice) (about 1 cup bread crumbs, reserving 2 teaspoons)

1 egg plus 1 egg white, lightly beaten

2 tablespoons evaporated skim milk

2 teaspoons low-sodium Worcestershire sauce

2 teaspoons lemon juice

½ teaspoon dry hot mustard

⅛ teaspoon ground oregano

⅛ teaspoon ground thyme

½ pound fresh lump crabmeat, picked over

2 teaspoons paprika

4 crab shells

Preheat the oven to 375°F.

Put the bread in a blender and process for 3 minutes, or until the crumbs are fine. In a large bowl, combine the 1 cup bread crumbs, egg plus egg white, milk, Worcestershire sauce, lemon juice, mustard, oregano and thyme; mix thoroughly. Gently fold in the crabmeat, being careful not to crumble it.

Spoon equal portions of the mixture into the crab shells and sprinkle each one with ½ *teaspoon* of the bread crumbs and ½ *teaspoon* of the paprika. Arrange the shells on a cookie sheet. Bake for 20 minutes. Serve hot.

PER SERVING	KCAL	FATgm	CHOLmg	SODmg
	104	2	92	578

NEW ORLEANS CRAB CAKES

MAKES 4 SERVINGS

WHEN MY EDITOR, Sandra, tasted these crab cakes, she said, "Enola, don't change a thing, I love them!"

1 *tablespoon reduced-calorie margarine*
2 *tablespoons finely chopped onions*
2 *tablespoons finely chopped green onions*
2 *tablespoons finely chopped fresh parsley*
½ *pound fresh lump crabmeat, picked over*
½ *cup fine dry bread crumbs*

1 *tablespoon prepared mustard*
1 *tablespoon low-sodium Worcestershire sauce*
¼ *teaspoon salt*
¼ *teaspoon granulated garlic*
¼ *teaspoon ground white pepper*
¼ *teaspoon ground red pepper*
1 *egg plus 1 egg white*

Preheat the oven to 375°F.

In a medium skillet over medium heat, melt the margarine. Add the onions, green onions and parsley and sauté for 3 minutes, stirring constantly. Add all the remaining ingredients except the egg and egg white; sauté for 1 minute. Remove the skillet from the heat and allow to cool slightly.

In a small bowl, beat the egg and egg white together. Add the beaten egg to the crabmeat mixture, stirring well to blend. Shape the crabmeat into 6 crab cakes, about ½-inch thick.

Spray the inside of a shallow baking pan with nonstick vegetable cooking spray. Place the crab cakes in the pan and bake for 15 minutes. Remove the pan from the oven, and use a spatula to turn the crab cakes. Bake for an additional 15 minutes, or until golden brown.

PER SERVING	KCAL	FATgm	CHOLmg	SODmg
	80	3	80	413

CRABMEAT AU GRATIN

MAKES 4 SERVINGS

1 tablespoon reduced-
   calorie margarine
1 cup finely chopped
   onions
½ cup finely chopped
   celery
¼ cup finely chopped
   green onions
3 tablespoons quick-
   mixing flour
1 cup evaporated skim
   milk
½ teaspoon ground red
   pepper

⅛ teaspoon ground white
   pepper
½ teaspoon salt
⅛ teaspoon ground
   oregano
1 pound fresh lump
   crabmeat, picked
   over
½ cup shredded reduced-
   fat Cheddar cheese
⅛ teaspoon paprika

Preheat the oven to 350°F. Spray four 12-ounce casseroles with
nonstick vegetable cooking spray.

In a large skillet over medium heat, melt the margarine. Add
the onions, celery and green onions; sauté, stirring occasionally,
for 5 minutes.

Dissolve the flour in the milk and add to the skillet with the red
and white peppers, salt and oregano. Cook for 15 minutes, or
until the sauce thickens, stirring constantly. Remove the skillet
from the heat and gently fold in the crabmeat just to mix. Spoon
the crabmeat mixture into the prepared casseroles. Top each with
the cheese and sprinkle with the paprika. Bake for 35 minutes,
or until brown and bubbly on top.

PER SERVING	KCAL	FATgm	CHOLmg	SODmg
	175	4.5	33	883

CRAB LIZZIE BETH

MAKES 8 SERVINGS

1 *cup low-fat cottage cheese*
1 *cup very finely chopped onions*
¼ *cup very finely chopped celery*
One *7¼-ounce can condensed tomato soup*
½ *teaspoon salt*
¼ *teaspoon ground white pepper*
¼ *teaspoon ground red pepper*
¼ *teaspoon ground oregano*

½ *pound fresh claw or lump crabmeat*
¼ *cup evaporated skim milk*
1 *tablespoon reduced-calorie soft-style cream cheese*
2 *tablespoons very finely chopped green onions*
1 *tablespoon unflavored gelatin*
2 *tablespoons water*
2 *tablespoons reduced-calorie mayonnaise*

In a blender, process the cottage cheese until smooth, reserving ¼ cup. Refrigerate the remaining cottage cheese for another use.

Spray a medium saucepan with nonstick vegetable cooking spray and place over high heat. Add the onions and celery; sauté for 10 minutes, stirring constantly to prevent burning. Reduce the heat to medium and add the tomato soup, salt, white and red peppers and oregano. Simmer for 10 minutes, stirring often.

Add the crabmeat, skim milk, cream cheese, green onions and ¼ cup blended cottage cheese; simmer, stirring for 5 minutes.

In a small bowl, sprinkle the gelatin in the water to dissolve. Remove the crabmeat from the heat and fold in the dissolved gelatin and mayonnaise, stirring well.

Spray a 6-cup mold with nonstick vegetable cooking spray. Spoon in the crabmeat mixture and refrigerate for 2 hours, or until firm.

PER SERVING	KCAL	FATgm	CHOLmg	SODmg
	8	1	29	394

MARINATED CRABFINGERS

MAKES 6 SERVINGS

JCRABFINGERS are cooked crab claws with all the shell removed except for one pincer on each claw. To eat them, hold the claw by the pincer with the shell and bite, pulling the meat off the tendon with your teeth. Feel free to experiment with your favorite spices in the marinade.

½ *cup finely chopped onions*

2 *teaspoons very finely chopped fresh parsley*

1 *teaspoon dried basil leaves, crushed*

1 *teaspoon dry hot mustard*

½ *teaspoon salt*

½ *teaspoon sugar*

¼ *teaspoon ground white pepper*

¼ *teaspoon ground oregano*

¼ *teaspoon ground red pepper*

⅓ *cup plus 1 tablespoon dry white wine*

3 *tablespoons balsamic vinegar*

2 *tablespoons peanut oil*

1 *tablespoon lime juice*

1 *pound cocktail crabfingers*

In a small bowl, combine all the ingredients except for the crabfingers, mixing well. Put the crabfingers in a medium bowl and pour in the marinade. Cover with plastic wrap and marinate at least 3 hours in the refrigerator, shaking the bowl several times while marinating. (Stirring will break up the crabfingers.) Drain the marinade before serving.

PER SERVING	KCAL	FATgm	CHOLmg	SODmg
	137	6	75	383

FABULOUS CRABMEAT CASSEROLE

MAKES 2 SERVINGS

FABULOUS is the only way to describe this dish!

1   *teaspoon reduced-calorie margarine*
½   *cup finely chopped onions*
1   *tablespoon all-purpose flour*
1½ *cups evaporated skim milk*
1   *teaspoon salt-free chicken bouillon granules*
½   *teaspoon granulated garlic*
¼   *teaspoon ground white pepper*

¼   *teaspoon ground oregano*
3   *tablespoons finely chopped green onions*
6   *ounces fresh lump crabmeat, picked over*
¼   *cup shredded part-skim mozzarella cheese*
Paprika

Preheat the oven to 375°F. Spray two 6-ounce casseroles with nonstick vegetable cooking spray.

In a large skillet over medium heat, melt the margarine. Add the onions and sauté for 3 to 4 minutes, stirring frequently to prevent sticking. Stir in the flour and continue cooking for 1 minute. Add the milk, bouillon, garlic, white pepper and oregano; continue to cook, stirring, for 5 minutes. Add the green onions and crabmeat and cook for 1 minute more.

Spoon the crabmeat mixture into the prepared casseroles. Top with the cheese and sprinkle with the paprika. Bake for 15 minutes, or until brown and bubbly. Serve hot.

PER SERVING	KCAL	FATgm	CHOLmg	SODmg
	311	5	53	927.6

SPICY CRAWFISH ETOUFFEE

MAKES 4 SERVINGS

THE WORD ÉTOUFFÉE means "smothered." The crawfish in this recipe are smothered in onions and bell peppers. The taste is fantastic!

2 tablespoons reduced-calorie margarine	⅛ teaspoon dried basil leaves, crushed
1½ cups finely chopped onions	One-half 6-ounce can condensed tomato paste
½ cup finely chopped green bell pepper	1½ cups Seafood Stock (page 19) or water
½ cup finely chopped celery	1 pound crawfish tails, peeled and deveined
1 teaspoon salt	¼ cup finely chopped green onions
1¼ teaspoons ground red pepper	2 tablespoons very finely chopped fresh parsley
1 teaspoon paprika	2 cups hot cooked rice
¼ teaspoon ground oregano	
⅛ teaspoon ground thyme	

In a medium saucepan over high heat, melt the margarine. Add the onions, bell pepper and celery; sauté stirring occasionally for 10 minutes. Add the salt, pepper, paprika, oregano, thyme and basil leaves, and cook for 5 minutes, stirring often.

Dissolve the tomato paste in the stock and add to the saucepan. Simmer for 10 minutes. Stir in the crawfish, green onions and parsley. Reduce the heat; cover and simmer for 10 minutes, stirring often. Remove from the heat and let stand, covered, for 5 minutes before serving. Serve over hot rice.

PER SERVING	KCAL	FATgm	CHOLmg	SODmg
	313	5	201	684

CRAWFISH CORN MAQUE CHOUX

MAKES 4 SERVINGS

IF CRAWFISH are unavailable, substitute shrimp or strips of chicken breast.

Two 10-ounce packages frozen whole-kernel corn
1 tablespoon reduced-calorie margarine
1 cup finely chopped onions
⅓ cup finely chopped green bell pepper
⅓ cup finely chopped celery

2 cups evaporated skim milk
1 cup Chicken Stock (page 20) or water
1 pound crawfish tails, peeled and deveined
⅓ cup finely chopped green onions
½ teaspoon salt
½ teaspoon ground white pepper

Place the corn in a food processor or blender and process until the kernels are chopped and resemble cream-style corn; set aside.

In a large Dutch oven over high heat, melt the margarine. Add the onions, bell pepper and celery and sauté for 10 minutes, stirring frequently. Reduce the heat to medium, and stir in the corn, milk and stock; cook, stirring frequently, for 15 minutes.

Spray the inside of a large skillet with nonstick vegetable cooking spray and place over high heat. Add the crawfish, green onions, salt and pepper; sauté for 5 minutes, then add the corn mixture. Simmer, covered, for 10 minutes, stirring often to prevent burning.

PER SERVING	KCAL	FATgm	CHOLmg	SODmg
	376	3.4	206	521

ENOLA'S CRAWFISH ENCHILADAS

MAKES 4 SERVINGS

3 tablespoons reduced-calorie margarine
1 cup finely chopped onions
⅓ cup chopped green bell pepper
1½ cups evaporated skim milk
½ cup reduced-calorie soft-style cream cheese
⅔ cup low-fat cottage cheese
½ teaspoon ground oregano
¼ teaspoon ground white pepper
½ cup peeled crawfish tails
2 tablespoons finely chopped green onions
2 tablespoons minced fresh jalapeño peppers
¼ cup shredded part-skim mozzarella cheese
4 corn tortillas

In a medium skillet over medium heat, melt the margarine. Add the onions and bell pepper and sauté for 5 minutes. Stir in the milk, cream cheese and cottage cheese; cook for 5 minutes, stirring constantly. Reduce the heat to simmer, and add the oregano, salt and white pepper; cook for an additional 5 minutes, stirring often to prevent burning.

Add the crawfish, green onions and jalapeños; simmer for 3 to 4 minutes. Add *half* the mozzarella and cook for 1 minute. Set aside.

In a small cast-iron skillet over medium heat, brown the tortillas for 1 minute on each side. Place each tortilla on a serving plate and divide the crawfish-cheese filling into equal portions and spoon into the middle of each tortilla; fold the tortillas in thirds across the filling and turn them seam side down. Top with the remaining filling, sprinkle on the remaining mozzarella cheese and serve immediately.

PER SERVING	KCAL	FATgm	CHOLmg	SODmg
	270	8	53	533

SHRIMP AND CRABMEAT JAMBALAYA

MAKES 4 SERVINGS

THE BLEND of seasonings in this jambalaya will make your taste buds go crazy!

2 *tablespoons reduced-calorie margarine*
1 *cup very finely chopped onions*
¼ *cup very finely chopped green bell pepper*
¼ *cup very finely chopped celery*
1 *cup chopped peeled and deveined small shrimp*
¼ *teaspoon salt*
¼ *teaspoon ground oregano*
¼ *teaspoon ground white pepper*

¼ *teaspoon ground red pepper*
¼ *teaspoon ground black pepper*
1⅓ *cups Chicken Stock (page 20) or water, in all*
1 *cup fresh claw crabmeat*
⅓ *cup very finely chopped green onions*
1 *tablespoon very finely chopped fresh parsley*
2 *cups cooked rice*

In a medium saucepan over high heat, melt margarine. Add the onions, bell pepper and celery and sauté for 5 minutes, stirring often. Add the shrimp, salt, oregano and white, red and black peppers; cook, stirring for 5 minutes. Add *1 cup* of the stock along with the crabmeat; cook for 5 minutes. Stir in the remaining stock, the green onions, parsley and rice, stirring to mix well. Cover and let stand for 10 minutes before serving.

PER SERVING	KCAL	FATgm	CHOLmg	SODmg
	210	2	125	593

STUFFED SHRIMP A LA CHRIS

MAKES 4 SERVINGS

THIS DISH is named after my daughter Stacie's husband, because he loves shrimp. This easy-to-make dish can be prepared a day ahead of serving; just keep it in the refrigerator until ready to bake.

½ teaspoon chili powder
¼ teaspoon ground white pepper
¼ teaspoon ground red pepper
⅛ teaspoon salt
⅛ teaspoon ground oregano
⅛ teaspoon ground thyme
12 large shrimp, peeled, deveined and butterflied
1 teaspoon low-sodium Worcestershire sauce
1 slice lean bacon, finely chopped
½ cup finely chopped onions

½ cup finely chopped green bell pepper
½ cup finely chopped celery
1 tablespoon salt-free chicken bouillon granules
½ cup water
⅓ cup finely chopped green onions
½ cup fine dry bread crumbs
1 tablespoon lemon juice
2 slices lean bacon, cut into ½-inch strips (12 pieces)

Preheat the oven to 350°F.

In a small bowl, combine the chili powder, white and red peppers, salt, oregano and thyme, mixing well. Put the shrimp in a medium bowl and toss with *1 teaspoon* of the seasoning mix and the Worcestershire sauce. Set aside the remaining seasoning.

In a large skillet over high heat, fry the finely chopped bacon until crisp. Add the onions, bell pepper and celery to the skillet and sauté for 3 minutes, stirring constantly. Dissolve the bouillon in the water. Add the bouillon and the green onions to the skillet. Cook, stirring constantly, for 5 minutes. Remove from the heat and stir in the bread crumbs, lemon juice and the remaining seasoning mix, stirring well to mix.

Allow the stuffing to cool to the touch, then stuff each shrimp with 1 tablespoon of the mixture. Wrap one bacon strip around each stuffed shrimp and secure with toothpicks. Arrange the shrimp on a baking sheet that has been sprayed with nonstick vegetable cooking spray. Bake for 15 minutes, or until the shrimp is done and the bacon is crispy. Remove the toothpicks before serving.

PER SERVING	KCAL	FATgm	CHOLmg	SODmg
	81	3	59	313

ENOLA'S BARBECUED SHRIMP

MAKES 2 SERVINGS

1 tablespoon reduced-calorie margarine

12 medium shrimp, peeled and deveined

½ teaspoon dried basil leaves, crushed

¼ teaspoon salt

¼ teaspoon ground oregano

⅛ teaspoon ground white pepper

⅛ teaspoon ground red pepper

⅛ teaspoon filé powder

1 tablespoon steak sauce

¼ cup finely chopped onions

½ cup light beer

In a large skillet over high heat, melt the margarine. Add the shrimp, basil, salt, oregano, white and red peppers and filé powder. Sauté for 3 minutes, or until the shrimp starts to stick to the bottom of the skillet, but stirring constantly to prevent burning. Add the remaining ingredients; cook, stirring, for 5 minutes, or until the sauce thickens. Serve hot.

PER SERVING	KCAL	FATgm	CHOLmg	SODmg
	100	3.5	83	543

BARBECUED SHRIMP DIANE

MAKES 2 SERVINGS

1 *tablespoon reduced-calorie margarine*

12 *medium shrimp, peeled and deveined*

⅛ *teaspoon ground white pepper*

⅛ *teaspoon ground oregano*

⅛ *teaspoon ground red pepper*

2 *tablespoons low-sodium catsup*

1 *tablespoon steak sauce*

2 *tablespoons low-sodium Worcestershire sauce*

½ *cup light beer*

In a large skillet over high heat, melt the margarine. Add the shrimp and sauté for 3 minutes, or until the shrimp starts to stick to the bottom of the skillet, but stirring constantly to prevent burning.

Add the remaining ingredients; cook, stirring for 5 minutes longer, or until the sauce thickens. Serve hot.

PER SERVING	KCAL	FATgm	CHOLmg	SODmg
	125	3.6	111	477

SHRIMP ETOUFFEE ACADIAN

MAKES 4 SERVINGS

*J*YEARS AGO the only place you could eat this was in a Cajun grandma's kitchen, but these days you can find it in kitchens everywhere. If this is the first time you're trying étouffée, you're in for a real treat!

1½ cups finely chopped onions	½ cup water
¾ cup finely chopped celery	2 cups Seafood Stock (page 19) or water
½ cup finely chopped green bell pepper	¼ cup finely chopped green onions
1 clove garlic, minced	3 tablespoons very finely chopped fresh parsley
¼ teaspoon ground white pepper	1 pound medium fresh shrimp, peeled and deveined
¼ teaspoon ground red pepper	1½ cups hot cooked rice
¼ teaspoon ground black pepper	
1 tablespoon tomato paste	

Spray the inside of a heavy saucepan with nonstick vegetable cooking spray and place over high heat. Add the onions, celery, bell pepper, garlic and white, red and black peppers, and sauté until the vegetables are tender and start to brown, about 10 minutes, stirring often to prevent sticking. Dissolve the tomato paste in the water; add to the saucepan with the stock and bring to a boil.

Reduce the heat to a simmer and cook, uncovered, for 25 minutes, stirring occasionally. Add the green onions, parsley and shrimp; cook for 5 minutes longer, or until the shrimp turn pink. Serve over hot rice.

PER SERVING	KCAL	FATgm	CHOLmg	SODmg
	231	1.5	221	286

SHRIMP CREOLE

MAKES 4 SERVINGS

J FIX THIS EASY, low-calorie version of a New Orleans favorite for someone special, who will think you slaved over a hot stove all day. The simplicity of this recipe will be your little secret!

1 *tablespoon reduced-calorie margarine*
2 *cups finely chopped onions*
½ *cup finely chopped green bell pepper*
⅓ *cup finely chopped celery*
2 *large tomatoes, peeled, seeded and chopped (about 1 cup)*
1 *clove garlic, minced*
2 *cups Seafood Stock (page 19) or water*
3 *tablespoons tomato paste*

1 *teaspoon salt*
1 *teaspoon paprika*
½ *teaspoon ground red pepper*
⅛ *teaspoon ground white pepper*
⅛ *teaspoon ground oregano*
⅛ *teaspoon ground thyme*
⅛ *teaspoon dried basil leaves, crushed*
½ *pound medium shrimp, peeled and deveined*
1 *cup hot cooked rice*

In a 6-quart pot over medium heat, melt the margarine. Add the onions, bell pepper and celery; sauté for 10 minutes, stirring frequently.

Add the remaining ingredients except for the shrimp and rice. Reduce the heat; simmer, covered, for 20 minutes, stirring frequently. Add the shrimp and cook, uncovered, for 10 minutes, or until the shrimp turn pink. Remove from the heat and let stand for 5 minutes before serving. Serve over hot rice.

PER SERVING	KCAL	FATgm	CHOLmg	SODmg
	123	2.6	110	310

SUNSET SHRIMP STEW

MAKES 4 SERVINGS

1 *cup chopped onions*
½ *cup chopped celery*
½ *cup chopped green bell pepper*
4 *cups Seafood Stock (page 19) or water*
1 *medium tomato, peeled and chopped (about ½ cup)*
½ *teaspoon salt*
¼ *teaspoon finely chopped dried dillweed*

⅛ *teaspoon ground oregano*
⅛ *teaspoon ground black pepper*
½ *cup Roux Flour (page 18)*
½ *pound medium shrimp, peeled and deveined*
20 *crabfingers*
⅓ *cup finely chopped green onions*
2 *tablespoons finely chopped fresh parsley*

Spray a large saucepan or Dutch oven with nonstick vegetable cooking spray and place over medium heat. Add the onions, celery and bell pepper and sauté for 10 minutes, stirring constantly to prevent burning. Add the stock, tomato, salt, dillweed, oregano, pepper and roux flour, stirring after each addition. Reduce to a simmer and stir until the roux flour is dissolved. Simmer, uncovered, for 20 minutes.

Add the shrimp and crabfingers; simmer, covered, for 10 minutes. Stir in the green onions and parsley. Remove the saucepan from the heat and let stand, covered, for 10 minutes before serving.

PER SERVING	KCAL	FATgm	CHOLmg	SODmg
	137	1	117	515

VEGETABLES AND SHRIMP PASTA

MAKES 2 SERVINGS

J THIS NO-FUSS DISH will become a regular in your kitchen. For a different twist, substitute with thin strips of chicken or turkey breast for the shrimp. Be creative and have fun with the recipes!

- 1 *cup low-fat cottage cheese*
- 12 *medium shrimp, peeled and deveined*
- 1 *small zucchini, thinly sliced (about 1 cup)*
- 1 *small carrot, shredded (about ½ cup)*
- ½ *cup finely chopped green onions*
- ¼ *teaspoon salt*
- ⅛ *teaspoon ground red pepper*
- 2 *cups cooked rotini (corkscrew-shaped pasta)*
- One *4-ounce can snap beans, drained*
- ½ *cup evaporated skim milk*

Place cottage cheese in a blender and process until smooth. Reserve ⅓ cup and refrigerate the rest for another use.

Spray the inside of a medium skillet with nonstick vegetable cooking spray and place over high heat. Add the shrimp, zucchini, carrot, green onions, salt and red pepper. Cook, stirring, for 8 minutes, or until the shrimp turn pink. Stir in the pasta and drained beans; cook, stirring, for 3 more minutes. Remove from the heat and transfer to a glass bowl; set aside.

To same skillet over high heat; add the milk and the reserved blended cottage cheese and bring to a boil. Cook, stirring, for 5 minutes, or until the sauce thickens, then add the shrimp and pasta mixture and cook for 1 minute more.

PER SERVING	KCAL	FATgm	CHOLmg	SODmg
	378	2.5	115	612

SHRIMP–HOT RICE CASSEROLE

MAKES 3 SERVINGS

THE HEARTY, robust flavor of this dish will make your taste buds come alive!

2 *tablespoons reduced-calorie margarine*
1 *cup finely chopped onions*
½ *cup finely chopped celery*
¼ *cup finely chopped green bell pepper*
2 *cloves garlic, minced*
⅛ *teaspoon salt*
⅛ *teaspoon ground white pepper*
⅛ *teaspoon ground red pepper*
1 *cup Seafood Stock (page 19) or water*

1 *pound medium shrimp, peeled and deveined*
½ *cup reduced-calorie cream of mushroom soup*
¼ *cup finely chopped green onions*
1 *tablespoon very finely chopped fresh parsley*
1½ *cups cooked rice*
¼ *cup fine dry bread crumbs*
1 *teaspoon paprika*

Preheat the oven to 375°F.

In a heavy large skillet over high heat, melt the margarine. Add the onions, celery, bell pepper, garlic, salt and white and red peppers. Reduce the heat to medium; sauté, stirring frequently, for 5 minutes. Stir in ½ cup of the stock, the shrimp and the mushroom soup; continue cooking, stirring, for 5 minutes. Add the remaining stock, green onions and parsley. Reduce the heat and simmer for 5 minutes. Fold in the rice, mixing well.

Spray a 2-quart casserole with nonstick vegetable cooking spray. Spoon the rice mixture into the casserole and sprinkle with the bread crumbs and paprika. Bake, uncovered, for 30 minutes, or until heated through. Serve hot.

PER SERVING	KCAL	FATgm	CHOLmg	SODmg
	241	5	111	571

SHRIMP, BROCCOLI AND RICE

MAKES 4 SERVINGS

THE CREAMY TEXTURE of the rice contrasted with the crunchy shrimp makes this a real palate pleaser!

1 *pound small shrimp, peeled and deveined*
2 *cups water*
1 *cup fresh broccoli florets*
1 *cup quick-cooking (not instant) rice*
1 *cup water*
One *10½-ounce can reduced-calorie cream of mushroom soup*

2 *tablespoons dehydrated onion*
¼ *teaspoon salt*
½ *teaspoon ground white pepper*

Spray a small skillet with nonstick vegetable cooking spray and place over high heat. Add the shrimp and sauté for 5 minutes, stirring often. Remove from the heat and set aside.

In a medium saucepan over high heat, bring 1 cup of the water to a boil. Add the broccoli and blanch for 3 minutes; drain and, when cool to the touch, chop coarsely.

Combine the shrimp, chopped broccoli, remaining 1 cup water, and all the remaining ingredients in the same saucepan over low heat. Stir well and cook, covered, for 30 minutes, or until the rice is tender.

PER SERVING	KCAL	FATgm	CHOLmg	SODmg
	244	1.3	83	543

good

SEAFOOD AND EGGPLANT CASSEROLE

MAKES 4 SERVINGS

1 *quart water*
3 *medium eggplants, peeled and coarsely cubed (about 5 cups)*
1 *tablespoon reduced-calorie margarine*
½ *pound medium shrimp, peeled and deveined*
1 *cup finely chopped onions*
½ *cup finely chopped green bell pepper*
½ *cup finely chopped celery*
1 *tablespoon lemon juice*
1 *teaspoon granulated garlic*
¼ *teaspoon salt*

½ *teaspoon ground oregano*
¼ *teaspoon ground white pepper*
¼ *teaspoon ground thyme*
½ *cup fresh lump crabmeat, picked over*
One *10-ounce can reduced-calorie cream of mushroom soup*
2 *slices bread (40 calories per slice), cut into ½-inch cubes*
⅓ *cup fine dry bread crumbs*
2 *teaspoons paprika*

Preheat the oven to 350°F.

In a large saucepan over high heat, combine the water and eggplant and bring to a boil; boil for 10 minutes, then drain and set aside.

In a medium skillet over medium heat, melt the margarine. Add the shrimp, onions, bell pepper, celery, lemon juice, garlic, salt, oregano, pepper and thyme, stirring well after each addition, and cook for 10 minutes. Remove from the heat, then stir in the eggplant, crabmeat, mushroom soup and bread crumbs.

Spray an 8-inch-square baking dish with vegetable cooking spray. Spoon the shrimp, crab and eggplant mixture in the prepared dish and top with the bread cubes and paprika. Bake for 30 minutes. Serve hot.

PER SERVING	KCAL	FATgm	CHOLmg	SODmg
	169	3	90	681

OYSTER AND POTATO STEW

MAKES 6 SERVINGS

HEARTY, dark brown stews are the heart and soul of a Cajun table—and this one is no exception.

1 *quart water*
1 *cup finely chopped onions*
½ *cup Roux Flour (page 18)*
⅓ *cup finely chopped green bell pepper*
⅓ *cup finely chopped celery*
1 *bay leaf*
½ *teaspoon salt*
1 *teaspoon granulated garlic*
¼ *teaspoon ground white pepper*

¼ *teaspoon ground red pepper*
¼ *teaspoon ground cumin*
1 *large potato, peeled and cut into 2-inch cubes*
½ *cup Seafood Stock (page 19) or water*
2 *cups drained oysters (about 24)*
⅓ *cup finely chopped green onions*
2 *tablespoons very finely chopped fresh parsley*

In a large pot over high heat, bring the water to a boil. Reduce the heat to medium and add the onions, roux flour, bell pepper, celery, bay leaf, salt, garlic, white and red peppers and cumin. Cover, and cook for 15 minutes, stirring occasionally. Add the potato cubes and stock; cook for 10 to 15 minutes, or until the potatoes are tender. Add the oysters, green onions and parsley; continue to cook, covered, for 5 minutes. Remove the bay leaf and serve hot.

PER SERVING	KCAL	FATgm	CHOLmg	SODmg
	129	2	0	256

BAKED OYSTERS AND EGGPLANT

MAKES 2 SERVINGS

½ teaspoon salt
1 teaspoon granulated garlic
1 teaspoon onion powder
1 teaspoon paprika
½ teaspoon ground red pepper
⅛ teaspoon ground white pepper
⅛ teaspoon ground oregano
⅛ teaspoon ground thyme
1 small eggplant, peeled and cut into ⅛-inch rounds
1 tablespoon reduced-calorie margarine
½ cup finely chopped green onions

½ cup thinly sliced fresh mushrooms
½ cup minced fresh onions
1 tablespoon quick-mixing flour
½ cup evaporated skim milk
¼ cup Seafood Stock (page 19) or water
1 dozen oysters, shucked and drained (about 1 cup)
2 tablespoons fine dry bread crumbs
2 tablespoons shredded part-skim mozzarella cheese
2 teaspoons very finely chopped fresh parsley

Preheat the oven to 350°F.

In a small bowl, combine the salt, garlic, onion powder, paprika, red and white peppers, oregano and thyme. Sprinkle *half* the seasoning mix on both sides of the eggplant.

Spray a medium skillet with nonstick vegetable cooking spray and place over high heat. Add the eggplant and sauté for 2 minutes, or until brown on both sides, turning often to prevent burning. Remove the eggplant slices and drain on paper towels. Spray two 6-ounce individual casseroles with nonstick vegetable cooking spray. Arrange the eggplant slices in the casseroles; set aside and keep warm.

In a medium skillet over high heat, melt the margarine. Stir in the green onions, mushrooms, minced onions, flour, milk, stock and the reserved seasoning. Reduce the heat to medium and cook for 10 minutes, stirring constantly. Add the oysters and cook for 5 minutes. Remove from the heat and divide the oyster mixture over the eggplant. Sprinkle half of the bread crumbs, cheese and parsley over each of the casseroles evenly and bake for 10 minutes. Serve hot.

PER SERVING	KCAL	FATgm	CHOLmg	SODmg
	267	7	7	805

OYSTER AND SPINACH CASSEROLE

MAKES 6 SERVINGS

One 10-ounce package
  frozen chopped spinach
1 tablespoon reduced-
  calorie margarine
½ cup very finely chopped
  onions
½ cup very finely chopped
  green onions
½ cup thinly sliced fresh
  mushrooms
½ teaspoon salt
1 teaspoon granulated
  garlic
½ teaspoon ground
  oregano

½ teaspoon ground thyme
24 medium oysters,
  shucked and drained
  (about 2 cups)
1 cup Seafood Stock
  (page 19) or water
¼ cup dry white wine
4 slices bread (40 calories
  per slice), cut into
  ½-inch cubes
¼ cup shredded part-skim
  mozzarella cheese
2 tablespoons fine dry
  bread crumbs
1 teaspoon paprika

Preheat the oven to 375°F.

Cook the spinach according to the directions on the package, omitting the salt. Drain the spinach and squeeze out the excess liquid. Spray an 8-inch-square baking dish with nonstick vegetable cooking spray. Add the spinach to the baking dish and set aside.

In a small skillet over high heat, melt the margarine. Add the onions, green onions and mushrooms; sauté for 5 minutes, stirring frequently. Add the salt, garlic, oregano and thyme and sauté for 5 minutes more, stirring constantly. Reduce the heat to medium and add the oysters, stock and wine.

Simmer for 5 minutes, or until the edges of the oysters start to curl. Remove the oyster mixture from the heat and spoon over the spinach, placing the oysters about ½ inch apart. Add the bread cubes. Top with the cheese, bread crumbs and paprika. Bake for 20 minutes. Serve hot.

PER SERVING	KCAL	FATgm	CHOLmg	SODmg
	148	4	4	430

FISH

SLIM-TRIM TROUT

MAKES 2 SERVINGS

I'M ESPECIALLY PROUD of this recipe because it was one of my first low-calorie creations!

1½ teaspoons ground red
    pepper
1 teaspoon paprika
¼ teaspoon salt
¼ teaspoon garlic powder
¼ teaspoon onion powder
¼ teaspoon ground
    oregano
¼ teaspoon ground thyme
1 pound trout fillets or
    any firm, white-
    fleshed fish

1 tablespoon olive oil
¼ cup chopped fresh
    mushrooms
¼ cup Seafood Stock
    (page 19) or water
1 tablespoon dry white
    wine
2 tablespoons finely
    chopped green
    onions

In a small bowl, mix together the red pepper, paprika, salt, garlic and onion powders, oregano and thyme. Sprinkle *half* the seasoning mix on both sides of the fish.

In a heavy skillet over high heat, heat the olive oil until very hot and then add the fish. Reduce the heat to medium and cook for 2 minutes, turning the fish once or twice. Add the mushrooms, stock, wine and the remaining seasoning mix; cook for 3 minutes, or until the mushrooms are tender. Add the green onions and cook for 1 minute, shaking skillet to keep the fish from burning. Serve hot.

PER SERVING	KCAL	FATgm	CHOLmg	SODmg
	269	7	83	396

OVEN-BARBECUED SEA TROUT

MAKES 4 SERVINGS

1 *pound sea trout fillets or any firm, white-fleshed fish*
1 *medium tomato, peeled, seeded and chopped (about ½ cup)*

½ *cup hickory-flavored barbecue sauce*
1 *tablespoon dehydrated onion*
1 *teaspoon dried basil leaves, crushed*

Preheat the oven to 350°F.

Spray an 8-inch-square baking dish with nonstick vegetable cooking spray. Arrange the fish in the baking dish. In a small bowl, combine the ingredients and pour over the fish. Cover with aluminum foil and bake for 30 minutes, or until the fish flakes easily with a fork.

PER SERVING	KCAL	FATgm	CHOLmg	SODmg
	203	5.5	82	295

FISH COURTBOUILLON

IT SEEMS like there are as many recipes for courtbouillon as there are Cajun families in South Louisiana. Some recipes call for a roux, others don't. (Mine does.) While catfish and redfish are commonly used, any firm, white-fleshed fish will do.

2 *tablespoons reduced-*
   calorie margarine
1 *cup chopped onions*
⅓ *cup chopped green bell*
   pepper
⅓ *cup chopped celery*
4 *medium tomatoes,*
   peeled, seeded and
   chopped (about 2
   cups)
½ *cup tomato paste*
2 *cups Seafood Stock*
   (page 19) or water

1 *teaspoon salt*
½ *teaspoon ground*
   oregano
¼ *teaspoon ground thyme*
¼ *teaspoon ground red*
   pepper
1 *pound fish fillets, cut*
   into 1-inch strips
½ *cup chopped green*
   onions
1 *tablespoon Roux Flour*
   (page 18)
3 *cups hot cooked rice*

In a 4-quart pot over medium heat, melt the margarine. Add the onions, bell pepper and celery, and sauté for 10 minutes, stirring frequently. Add the tomatoes, tomato paste, stock, salt, oregano, thyme and red pepper and stir well. Reduce the heat and simmer, covered, for 20 minutes. Add the fish, green onions and roux flour; stir well. Simmer, covered, for 20 minutes. Shake the pot occasionally to prevent sticking, but do not stir, as that will cause the fish to break up. Serve hot over cooked rice.

PER SERVING	KCAL	FATgm	CHOLmg	SODmg
	156	3	35	441

HOT AND TANGY RED SNAPPER

MAKES 4 SERVINGS

1 *teaspoon granulated garlic*
¼ *teaspoon salt*
¼ *teaspoon ground white pepper*
¼ *teaspoon ground red pepper*
¼ *teaspoon ground oregano*
¼ *teaspoon ground thyme*
1 *pound red snapper fillets or any firm, white-fleshed fish*

½ *cup unsweetened orange juice*
½ *cup hickory-flavored barbecue sauce*
2 *tablespoons lemon juice*
2 *tablespoons lime juice*
1 *tablespoon honey*
1 *tablespoon dehydrated onion*
2 *tablespoons very finely chopped green onions*
2 *tablespoons very finely chopped fresh parsley*

Preheat the oven to 350°F.

In a small bowl, mix together the garlic, salt, white and red peppers, oregano and thyme. Sprinkle the seasoning mixture on both sides of the fish. Spray an 8-inch-square baking dish with nonstick vegetable cooking spray. Arrange the fish fillets in the dish and set aside.

In a small saucepan over high heat, bring to a boil the remaining ingredients except for the green onions and parsley. Boil for 10 minutes, stirring often. Remove the sauce from heat, spoon over the fish, then top with the green onions and parsley. Bake, uncovered, for 20 minutes, or until the fish flakes easily with a fork.

PER SERVING	KCAL	FATgm	CHOLmg	SODmg
	179	2	41	821

SNAPPER VERMILION A LA BRADY

MAKES 4 SERVINGS

½ teaspoon salt
½ teaspoon chili powder
¼ teaspoon granulated garlic
¼ teaspoon ground oregano
¼ teaspoon ground thyme
¼ teaspoon ground red pepper
¼ teaspoon ground black pepper
½ pound red snapper fillets or other firm, white-fleshed fish
6 medium shrimp, peeled and deveined
1 cup finely chopped onions

½ cup thinly sliced fresh mushrooms
½ cup finely chopped celery
¼ cup finely chopped green onions
2 tablespoons tomato paste
1 cup Chicken Stock (page 20) or water
2 large tomatoes, peeled, seeded and chopped (about 1 cup)
1 tablespoon prepared low-sodium mustard
¼ teaspoon brown sugar substitute
¼ teaspoon liquid smoke

Preheat the oven to 350°F.

In a small bowl, mix together the salt, chili powder, garlic, oregano, thyme and red and black peppers. Sprinkle *half* the seasoning mixture on the fish and shrimp. Reserve the remaining seasoning. Spray an 8-inch-square baking dish with nonstick vegetable cooking spray. Arrange the fish fillets in the dish and set aside.

Spray the inside of a medium skillet with nonstick vegetable cooking spray and place over high heat. Add the shrimp, onions, mushrooms, celery and green onions; sauté for 5 minutes, stirring frequently. Transfer the shrimp and vegetables to a dish and set aside. In the same skillet, heat the stock and dissolve the tomato

paste. Add the chopped tomatoes. Cook, stirring, for 10 minutes. Add the mustard, sugar substitute, liquid smoke and remaining seasoning mix; cook, stirring for 5 minutes more.

Arrange 3 shrimp on top of each fish fillet, then top with the sauce. Cover with aluminum foil and bake for 15 minutes. Uncover, and bake for an additional 15 minutes, or until the fish flakes easily with a fork.

PER SERVING	KCAL	FATgm	CHOLmg	SODmg
	115	1.5	48	587

SNAPPER FLORENTINE A LA RAY

MAKES 2 SERVINGS

¼ teaspoon salt
½ teaspoon chili powder
¼ teaspoon granulated
    garlic
¼ teaspoon ground
    oregano
¼ teaspoon ground thyme
¼ teaspoon ground red
    pepper
¼ teaspoon ground black
    pepper

½ pound red snapper
    fillets or any firm,
    white-fleshed fish
One 10-ounce package
    frozen chopped spinach,
    thawed
2 tablespoons dehydrated
    onion
½ cup Seafood Stock
    (page 19) or water
½ cup evaporated skim
    milk

Preheat the oven to 350°F.

In a small bowl, mix together the salt, chili powder, garlic, oregano, thyme and red and black peppers. Sprinkle *half* the seasoning mix on both sides of the fish; reserve the remaining seasoning and set aside. Spray an 8-inch-square baking dish with nonstick vegetable cooking spray and set the dish aside.

Spray a medium skillet with nonstick vegetable cooking spray and place over high heat. Add the spinach and dehydrated onion; and cook for 5 minutes, stirring frequently.

Add the stock, ¼ cup of the milk, and the remaining seasoning mix. Cook, stirring for 5 minutes or until all the liquid has evaporated. Transfer the spinach mixture to the prepared baking dish and set aside.

Spray both sides of the fish fillets with the nonstick vegetable cooking spray and place on a hot flat grill or in a cast-iron skillet. Cook the fish for 3 minutes on each side, turning with a spatula. Arrange the fish on top of the spinach and top with the remaining milk. Cover the dish with aluminum foil and bake for 15 minutes.

PER SERVING	KCAL	FATgm	CHOLmg	SODmg
	210	2	44	521

BAKED GROUPER CREOLE

MAKES 4 SERVINGS

1 *pound (½ inch thick) grouper fillets or other lean, white-fleshed fish*

1 *tablespoon low-sodium Worcestershire sauce*

½ *teaspoon paprika*

¼ *teaspoon ground white pepper*

¼ *teaspoon ground red pepper*

¼ *teaspoon garlic powder*

¼ *teaspoon dried dillweed*

1 *tablespoon reduced-calorie margarine*

1 *cup finely chopped onions*

¼ *cup finely chopped green bell pepper*

¼ *cup finely chopped celery*

1 *cup Chicken Stock (page 20) or water*

1 *medium tomato, peeled, seeded and chopped (about ½ cup)*

Preheat the oven to 350°F.

Spray an 8-inch-square baking dish with nonstick vegetable cooking spray. Arrange the fish fillets in the baking dish and sprinkle with the Worcestershire sauce. In a small bowl, mix together the paprika, white and red peppers, garlic powder and dillweed, and sprinkle on both sides of the fish. Set aside.

In a small skillet over high heat, melt the margarine. Add the onions, bell pepper and celery; sauté, stirring for 5 minutes. Add the stock and cook for 5 minutes more, stirring often. Reduce the heat to medium; add the tomatoes and simmer for 3 minutes. Remove the sauce from the heat and pour over the fish. Bake for 30 minutes or until the fish flakes easily with a fork.

PER SERVING	KCAL	FATgm	CHOLmg	SODmg
	174	3	53	121

ZESTY LEMON CATFISH

MAKES 4 SERVINGS

THIS DISH has a mild, tangy lemon flavor. If you don't have dried lemon peel, use a lemon-pepper seasoning.

1 *teaspoon dried or fresh*
    lemon peel
¼ *teaspoon salt*
¼ *teaspoon granulated*
    garlic
¼ *teaspoon paprika*
Two 8-ounce catfish fillets
    or any firm, white-
    fleshed fish

1 *teaspoon very finely*
    chopped fresh parsley
½ *small lemon, thinly*
    sliced

Preheat a flat grill.
In a small bowl, combine the lemon peel, salt, garlic and paprika. Mix well and sprinkle on both sides of the fish. Spray the grill with nonstick vegetable cooking spray and place the fish on the hot grill. Grill the fish on one side for 4 minutes, turn, and grill the fish for 6 minutes on the other side. Transfer the fish to warm serving plates, garnish with parsley and lemon slices and serve.

PER SERVING	KCAL	FATgm	CHOLmg	SODmg
	138	2.4	61	232

BLACKENED CATFISH

MAKES 1 SERVING

⨍ MY SON SONNY AYMOND, who is one of our chefs at the Cajun Cafe, says, "My uncle, Chef Paul Prudhomme, who made blackened fish so popular, shared his technique with me when Mama opened her restaurant. We serve the original version of this dish daily. It's such a popular item, I decided to create this low-calorie version."

½ teaspoon paprika
⅛ teaspoon salt
¼ teaspoon ground red pepper
¼ teaspoon ground cumin
¼ teaspoon ground thyme

⅛ teaspoon ground white pepper
One 4-ounce catfish fillet or any firm, white-fleshed fish

Preheat the oven to 350°F. Spray a baking sheet with nonstick vegetable cooking spray and set aside.

Place a medium cast-iron skillet over high heat for 15 minutes. While the skillet is heating, combine the seasonings in a small bowl and set aside.

Spray both sides of the fish with nonstick vegetable cooking spray and sprinkle one side with *half* the seasoning. Place the seasoned side down in the skillet and cook for 1½ minutes.

While the fish is cooking on one side quickly sprinkle the remaining seasoning on the other side. Using a spatula, turn the fish and cook for 1½ minutes on the other side. Remove the fish from the skillet and place on the prepared baking sheet. Bake for 5 minutes, or until the fish flakes easily with a fork.

PER SERVING	KCAL	FATgm	CHOLmg	SODmg
	146	2.6	61	355

CAJUN CATFISH

MAKES 3 SERVINGS

⅛ teaspoon butter-flavored granules
⅛ teaspoon ground white pepper
⅛ teaspoon ground oregano
⅛ teaspoon ground thyme
⅛ teaspoon paprika
Dash ground red pepper
1 tablespoon reduced-calorie margarine

Two 3-to-5-ounce catfish fillets
1 cup thinly sliced fresh mushrooms
¼ cup finely chopped green onions
2 tablespoons dry white wine
½ cup beef stock or water

In a small bowl, combine first 6 ingredients and mix together well. Sprinkle the seasoning mixture on both sides of the fish and set aside.

In a large skillet over high heat, melt the margarine until bubbly. Add the fish and sauté for 1 minute, or until the fish is lightly browned, turning often. Add the mushrooms and green onions and cook for another minute.

Add the wine and cook for 5 minutes, or until the fish flakes easily with a fork and the mushrooms are tender, shaking the skillet often. Add the stock and cook for 3 minutes. When the liquid is reduced by half, remove fillets using a spatula and place them on warm serving plates.

Over high heat continue reducing the sauce for 3 minutes, or until it reaches a thick, rich, consistency. Remove from the heat and spoon some sauce over each fillet.

PER SERVING	KCAL	FATgm	CHOLmg	SODmg
	146	4	51	145

OVEN-FRIED GARFISH BALLS

MAKES 20 BALLS OR 4 TO 5 MAIN-DISH SERVINGS

2 *cups water*
1 *medium potato, peeled and cut into ½-inch cubes*
2 *pounds garfish steaks*
½ *cup very finely chopped onions*
¼ *cup very finely chopped green bell pepper*
¼ *cup very finely chopped celery*

¼ *cup very finely chopped green onions*
1 *egg plus 2 egg whites*
1 *teaspoon salt*
1 *teaspoon paprika*
½ *teaspoon ground red pepper*
½ *cup fine dry bread crumbs*

Preheat the oven to 400°F. Spray a large baking sheet with nonstick vegetable cooking spray.

In a medium saucepan over high heat, bring the water to a boil. Add the potato and boil for 10 minutes, or until tender when pierced with a fork. Drain and set aside.

Place the fish on a clean, flat surface. Hold the bone end of the steak with the left hand while pulling the fish flesh away from the bone with a fork, pulling outward, away from bone. Reserve the fish flesh and discard the bones.

In a large bowl, combine the potato, fish and the remaining ingredients except for the bread crumbs. Mix well and shape into 1½-inch balls. Roll the balls in the bread crumbs and place them on the baking sheet approximately 1 inch apart. Bake for 30 minutes, or until brown.

No nutritional information available.

CATFISH AU GRATIN

MAKES 4 SERVINGS

½ cup Seafood Stock (page 19) or water
½ cup dry sherry
½ cup evaporated skim milk
¼ teaspoon salt
⅛ teaspoon ground white pepper
⅛ teaspoon ground red pepper
⅛ teaspoon granulated garlic
⅛ teaspoon ground oregano
1 pound catfish fillets
2 tablespoons shredded part-skim mozzarella cheese
2 tablespoons fine dry bread crumbs
Paprika

Preheat the oven to 375°F.

Spray a medium saucepan with nonstick vegetable cooking spray. In the saucepan, combine the stock, sherry, milk, salt, white and red peppers, garlic and oregano. Place over high heat and bring to a boil. Boil for 2 minutes, stirring often. Reduce the heat to medium and simmer for 2 minutes, or until the sauce thickens.

Spray an 8-inch-square baking dish with nonstick vegetable cooking spray. Arrange the fish in the dish and pour the sauce on top. Sprinkle with the cheese and bread crumbs, then the paprika. Bake for 20 minutes. Transfer the fish to a warm serving platter and top with the sauce.

PER SERVING	KCAL	FATgm	CHOLmg	SODmg
	208	3.7	66.7	314

CATFISH WITH MUSTARD-WINE SAUCE

MAKES 6 SERVINGS

Three 8-ounce catfish
    fillets
2 teaspoons paprika
1 teaspoon granulated
    garlic
½ teaspoon salt
½ teaspoon ground
    oregano
½ teaspoon dried basil
    leaves, crushed

½ teaspoon ground red
    pepper
¼ teaspoon ground black
    pepper
⅓ cup dry white wine
2 tablespoons Dijon
    mustard
1 tablespoon low-sodium
    Worcestershire sauce
¼ teaspoon liquid smoke

Wash the fish and pat dry. Using a sharp knife, make three half-inch diagonal slits across each side of the fish. In a small bowl, combine the paprika, garlic, salt, oregano, basil and red and black peppers. Sprinkle the seasoning mixture on the outside and inside the cavities of each fish.

In a small bowl, combine wine, mustard, Worcestershire sauce and liquid smoke; mix well. Spray an 8-inch-square baking dish with nonstick vegetable cooking spray. Arrange the fish in the dish and pour the sauce over it. Cover and refrigerate for at least 3 hours.

Preheat the oven to 375°F. Bake the fish, covered, for 15 minutes. Turn the fish and baste with the pan juices; bake, uncovered, for another 15 minutes, or until the fish flakes easily with a fork.

PER SERVING	KCAL	FATgm	CHOLmg	SODmg
	158	3	3	359

ALLIGATOR GARFISH IN WHITE SAUCE

MAKES 2 SERVINGS

*J*GARFISH is popular in South Louisiana. While several different varieties are fished from our local bayous, the most common one is known as the alligator gar. With its long, pointed head and very sharp teeth the garfish resemble the alligator found in the swamps. Smaller garfish is favored when grilling or barbecuing, use larger steaks for pan-frying.

1½ *teaspoons salt*
½ *teaspoon granulated garlic*
½ *teaspoon ground white pepper*
½ *teaspoon ground red pepper*
2 *whole garfish steaks (about ½ pound each) or any firm, white-fleshed fish*
1 *tablespoon reduced-calorie margarine*
3 *tablespoons all-purpose flour*

1 *cup finely chopped onions*
½ *cup finely chopped green bell pepper*
½ *cup finely chopped celery*
2 *cups Seafood Stock (page 19) or water*
½ *cup finely chopped green onions*
2 *tablespoons very finely chopped fresh parsley*
1 *cup hot cooked rice*

In a small bowl, mix together the salt, garlic and white and red peppers. Sprinkle the seasoning mixture on both sides of the fish; set aside.

In a large skillet over high heat, melt the margarine. Add the flour, onions, bell pepper and celery and sauté for 5 minutes, stirring constantly. Reduce the heat and add the stock and fish; cover, and simmer for 20 minutes or until the fish is tender. Gently add the green onions and parsley, taking care not break up the fish. Remove from heat and let stand for 10 minutes before serving over hot rice.

No nutritional information available.

CITRUS SHARK

MAKES 4 SERVINGS

Two 8-ounce shark fillets,
  quartered
1 teaspoon granulated
  garlic
1 teaspoon dried lemon
  peel
1 teaspoon paprika
1 teaspoon dried
  rosemary leaves,
  crushed
¼ teaspoon salt
½ cup dry white wine
2 tablespoons orange
  liqueur, such as
  Grand Marnier

2 teaspoons cornstarch
½ cup evaporated skim
  milk
1 tablespoon reduced-
  calorie margarine
1 tablespoon dehydrated
  onion
One ¾-ounce slice
  reduced-fat American-
  cheese product,
  shredded

Place the fish pieces in a baking dish. In a small bowl, combine the garlic, lemon peel, paprika, rosemary and salt; sprinkle over the fish. Add the wine and liqueur, then cover and refrigerate for 8 hours or overnight.

The next day, preheat the oven to 350°F. Drain the fish, reserving the marinade. Dissolve the cornstarch in the milk and set aside. In a small skillet over medium heat, melt the margarine. Add the reserved marinade, the dissolved cornstarch, and the onion; cook for 5 minutes, stirring often. Add the cheese and stir constantly until melted. Remove from the heat and pour over the fish. Bake for 20 minutes, or until the fish flakes easily with a fork.

PER SERVING	KCAL	FATgm	CHOLmg	SODmg
	233	7.7	59	406

HALIBUT STEAKS WITH LEMON

MAKES 4 SERVINGS

1 *pound halibut steaks*
½ *teaspoon plus ⅛*
   teaspoon paprika
¼ *teaspoon salt*
¼ *teaspoon granulated*
   garlic
¼ *teaspoon ground red*
   pepper
⅛ *teaspoon dried dillweed*

1 *tablespoon reduced-*
   calorie margarine
½ *small lemon, thinly*
   sliced
1 *cup evaporated skim*
   milk
1 *tablespoon lemon juice*
2 *tablespoons very finely*
   chopped green onions

Preheat the oven to 350°F.

Spray an 8-inch-square baking dish with nonstick vegetable cooking spray. Arrange the fish in the baking dish and set aside. In a small bowl, combine the ½ *teaspoon* paprika, salt, garlic, red pepper and dillweed; sprinkle the seasoning mixture on the fish; set aside.

In a small skillet over high heat, melt the margarine. Add the lemon slices and sauté for 3 minutes, stirring often. Remove the lemon from the skillet and set aside. Stir the milk and lemon juice into the skillet and cook for 3 minutes, or until the sauce thickens. Stir in the green onions and pour the sauce over the fish. Arrange the lemon slices on top of the fish and sprinkle on the remaining paprika. Bake for 30 minutes, or until the fish flakes easily with a fork.

PER SERVING	KCAL	FATgm	CHOLmg	SODmg
	227	5	49	309

SALMON WITH CREOLE MUSTARD

MAKES 4 SERVINGS

½ cup plus 2 tablespoons
plain low-fat yogurt
2 tablespoons Creole
mustard
2 teaspoons reduced-
calorie mayonnaise
2 teaspoons lemon juice
1 tablespoon dry white
wine

¼ teaspoon hot pepper
sauce
¼ teaspoon salt
Four 4-ounce salmon
steaks
⅛ teaspoon salt
⅛ teaspoon ground red
pepper
1 teaspoon lemon juice

Preheat a coal or gas grill.

In a blender, or food processor, combine the yogurt, mustard, mayonnaise, lemon juice, wine, pepper sauce and the ¼ teaspoon of salt and blend until smooth. Put the mustard sauce in a serving dish; cover, and chill for 1 hour.

Sprinkle the fish with the ⅛ teaspoon salt, red pepper and lemon juice. Grill the fish for 5 minutes on each side, or until the fish flakes easily with a fork. Transfer the salmon to warm serving plates and serve with the mustard sauce.

PER SERVING	KCAL	FATgm	CHOLmg	SODmg
	242	10	59	380

SALMON TERRINE A LA SHELTON

MAKES 6 SERVINGS

THIS DISH is named for my husband, Shelton, who could eat fish seven days a week.

¼ cup Seafood Stock (page 19) or water
¼ cup dry white wine
⅛ teaspoon salt
One 6-ounce salmon fillet
⅓ cup finely chopped celery
¼ cup finely chopped onions
¼ cup finely chopped green bell pepper

¼ cup finely chopped red bell pepper
1 teaspoon granulated garlic
1 egg plus 2 egg whites
⅛ cup evaporated skim milk
1 slice bread (40 calories per slice), toasted and made into crumbs (about ¼ cup)

Preheat the oven to 350°F. Spray an 8-by-4-by-2-inch loaf pan with nonstick vegetable cooking spray and set aside.

In a medium skillet over high heat, combine the stock, wine and salt and bring to a boil. Reduce the heat to medium; add the fish and simmer, covered, for 6 minutes, or until the fish flakes easily with a fork, turning once. Remove the skillet from the heat. Using a slotted spoon, transfer the fish to a medium bowl, reserving the cooking liquid in another bowl. Flake the fish with a fork and set aside.

Spray the same skillet with nonstick vegetable cooking spray and place over high heat. Add the celery, onions, green and red bell peppers and garlic; sauté for 3 minutes, stirring frequently, or until the onion is tender. Remove the vegetable mixture from the heat and add it to the fish. In a small bowl, using a fork,

beat together the egg, egg whites and milk. Gradually add the beaten egg to the fish mixture. Stir in the reserved liquid, mixing thoroughly well. Stir in the bread crumbs.

Using a spatula, scrape the fish mixture into the prepared pan, and cover with aluminum foil. Place the loaf pan in a larger, shallow baking pan in the oven. Pour one inch of hot water into the larger pan. Bake for 45 minutes, or until the center of the fish mixture is firm. Allow the terrine to cool. Using a spatula, loosen the edges and invert onto a serving platter. Garnish with lemon slices if desired. Slice into 1-inch serving pieces. Serve warm or chilled.

PER SERVING	KCAL	FATgm	CHOLmg	SODmg
	94	3	59	122

PINK SALMON ANNETTE

MAKES 6 SERVINGS

WHEN I WAS A CHILD, we didn't eat meat on Fridays, so Mama would fix this dish often. My daughter Annette loves salmon, so I named this dish after her. It's simple to prepare and you don't have to wait until Fridays come around to enjoy it!

2 tablespoons reduced- calorie margarine	½ cup finely chopped green onions
2 cups finely chopped onions	2 tablespoons finely chopped fresh parsley
½ cup finely chopped green bell pepper	¼ teaspoon ground white pepper
½ cup finely chopped celery	¼ teaspoon ground red pepper
1½ cups Seafood Stock (page 19) or water	¼ teaspoon ground oregano
⅓ cup tomato paste	¼ teaspoon ground thyme
One 15½-ounce can pink salmon, drained	3 cups hot cooked rice

In a medium saucepan over high heat, melt the margarine. Add the onions, bell pepper and celery; sauté for 10 minutes, stirring frequently. Reduce the heat to medium; add the stock and tomato paste and cook for 5 minutes.

Add the salmon, green onions, parsley, white and red peppers, oregano and thyme. Reduce the heat, and simmer for an additional 10 minutes. Shake the saucepan often to prevent sticking; do not stir, as that will cause the salmon to break up. Serve over hot rice.

PER SERVING	KCAL	FATgm	CHOLmg	SODmg
	247	7	0.16	476

BAKED ORANGE ROUGHY

MAKES 4 SERVINGS

PARCHMENT PAPER is moisture-resistant paper that is ideal for cooking fish because it seals in the juices and keeps the fish from falling apart. Try using parchment paper with any of the baked fish dishes in this book. You can use aluminum foil, but it doesn't look as nice.

1 *tablespoon dehydrated onion*
¼ *teaspoon salt*
½ *teaspoon ground white pepper*
½ *teaspoon dried basil leaves, crushed*
¼ *teaspoon ground oregano*
1 *pound orange roughy fillets* or *any firm white-fleshed fish, divided into 2 pieces*

2 *tablespoons hickory-flavored barbecue sauce*
1 *tablespoon lemon juice*
1 *teaspoon prepared horseradish*

Preheat the oven to 375°F. Tear off two 12-inch pieces of parchment paper, place on a baking sheet and set aside.

In a small bowl, combine the onion, salt, pepper, basil and oregano. Mix well and sprinkle on both sides of the fish. Place each piece of fish on one-half of each piece of parchment paper on the baking sheet.

In a small bowl, combine the barbecue sauce, lemon juice and horseradish. Pour the sauce on the fish. Fold the parchment over the fish and seal by making small folds all the way around. Bake for 20 minutes. To serve, remove the entire package to a serving plate, fold back the paper and enjoy!

PER SERVING	KCAL	FATgm	CHOLmg	SODmg
	148	2.5	61	248

ORANGE ROUGHY WITH PECAN SAUCE

MAKES 4 SERVINGS

A VERY POPULAR high-calorie version of this dish is served in the restaurant, but I wanted everyone to enjoy it, so I changed a few ingredients and came up with this mouth-watering masterpiece!

½ teaspoon salt
1 teaspoon paprika
½ teaspoon ground red pepper
¼ teaspoon ground black pepper
¼ teaspoon dried basil leaves, crushed
¼ teaspoon ground oregano
¼ teaspoon ground thyme
1 pound orange roughy fillets or any firm, white-fleshed fish, divided into 2 pieces

1 tablespoon reduced-calorie margarine
1 tablespoon reduced-calorie soft-style cream cheese
2 tablespoons pecan meal (page 15)
1 tablespoon very finely chopped onions
1 teaspoon lemon juice
¼ teaspoon granulated garlic

Preheat a coal or gas grill.

In a small bowl, combine the salt, paprika, red and black peppers, basil, oregano and thyme. Mix well and sprinkle on both sides of the fish.

In a small bowl, combine the margarine and cream cheese, mixing well. Add the pecan meal, onions, lemon juice and garlic, stirring until mixed.

Spray the fish on both sides with nonstick vegetable cooking spray. Grill for 4 minutes on each side. On 2 warm serving plates, place *1 tablespoon* of the sauce in the center of each. Add the fish and top each one with half of the remaining sauce.

PER SERVING	KCAL	FATgm	CHOLmg	SODmg
	187	6	63	375

POULTRY

TURKEY SAUCE PIQUANT

MAKES 4 SERVINGS

SERVE THIS AS IS or over pasta or rice.

1 *pound turkey breast, cut into 1-inch strips*
½ *teaspoon salt*
¼ *teaspoon granulated garlic*
⅛ *teaspoon ground white pepper*
1 *cup chopped onions*
3 *cups Chicken Stock (page 20) or water*
3 *medium tomatoes, peeled, seeded and chopped (about 1½ cups)*

2 *tablespoons tomato paste*
1 *tablespoon very finely chopped jalapeño peppers*
1 *tablespoon Roux Flour (page 18)*

Spray a 4-quart pot with nonstick vegetable cooking spray and place over medium heat. Add the turkey, salt, garlic and white pepper; cook for 5 minutes, or until the turkey loses its color, stirring constantly to prevent burning. Add the onions and cook for 10 minutes, stirring frequently. Add ½ cup of the stock, the tomatoes, tomato paste, jalapeños, roux flour and remaining stock, mixing after each addition. Reduce heat to simmer; cover and cook for 15 minutes.

PER SERVING	KCAL	FATgm	CHOLmg	SODmg
	199	2	5	354

TURKEY TASSO

MAKES ABOUT 2½ POUNDS

*T*ASSO is a highly seasoned smoked ham used in gumbos, stuffings, and bean or pasta dishes. I developed this version made with turkey instead of pork. Plan ahead when making turkey tasso—the meat marinates for 2 days and smokes for 1.

2 *tablespoons sugar*
2 *tablespoons granulated garlic*
2 *tablespoons onion powder*
2 *tablespoons ground red pepper*
2 *tablespoons ground black pepper*
2 *tablespoons paprika*

1 *tablespoon ground white pepper*
2 *teaspoons salt*
1 *tablespoon ground cumin*
3 *pounds skinned and boned turkey breast*
2 *tablespoons liquid smoke*

In a small bowl, combine the sugar, garlic, onion powder, red, white and black peppers, paprika, salt and cumin, mixing well. Place the turkey breast in a large glass bowl and sprinkle with 4 *tablespoons* of the seasoning mix, coating well. (Store the remaining seasoning in a covered container for another use.)

Sprinkle the turkey with liquid smoke, rubbing the seasoning and liquid over the entire turkey breast. Cover the bowl and marinate for 2 days, in the refrigerator turning the turkey over several times while marinating.

Light the charcoal in a water smoker, cover, and let the heat and smoke accumulate. When the smoker is ready, place the turkey breast on the wire rack and smoke for 7 hours. Add water to the smoker as needed. Add a few mesquite chips to the charcoal every hour or two.

When the tasso is done, remove and set aside until cool enough to handle. Store in plastic freezer bags, removing as much as possible, up to 1 month in the refrigerator or 6 months in the freezer.

PER ½POUND	KCAL	FATgm	CHOLmg	SODmg
	434	3	227	931

SMOKED TURKEY SAUSAGE

MAKES ABOUT 3 POUNDS

ANDOUILLE is the most popular Cajun smoked pork sausage, but turkey sausage is much lower in fat and calories, so I use it in all my low-calorie recipes. Turkey sausage is now available in supermarkets, but if you would like to try your hand at making your own, here's how. You can also buy turkey sausage and smoke it yourself.

I've included two methods for making sausage; you can use sausage casings (small quantities are readily available in many supermarkets) or aluminum foil if casings are not available.

Sausage casings
3½ pounds boneless turkey breast
½ pound potatoes, peeled and quartered
1 teaspoon salt
1 tablespoon paprika
1½ teaspoons ground red pepper

1 teaspoon ground white pepper
1 teaspoon granulated garlic
½ teaspoon ground sage
¼ teaspoon ground nutmeg
2 teaspoons liquid smoke

Following the manufacturer's directions, light the smoker, cover and allow the heat and smoke to accumulate.

In a meat grinder or food processor, grind together the turkey and potatoes until coarsely ground. Transfer to a mixing bowl and add the remaining ingredients, mixing thoroughly. Refrigerate until ready to use.

Sausage-Casings Method: Soak the sausage casings for 1 hour in a small bowl with enough water to cover. Rinse the casings thoroughly to remove the excess salt. Running water through the casings will indicate if there are any holes in the casings. If holes or leaks are found, discard the casing. Place one of the casings on a sausage horn stuffer, taking care not to tear it, tie a knot in the other end and stuff the casing with the turkey mixture. When stuffed, tie a knot to enclose the open end. Place the sausage on the rack in the smoker and smoke for 2 hours. Turn the sausage and smoke for an additional 2 hours.

Aluminum-Foil Method: Tear off two 20-inch pieces of aluminum foil. Place half the turkey mixture lengthwise on each piece of foil 3 inches from the edge. Roll the foil tightly to form a log. Place the sausage on the rack in the smoker and smoke for 2 hours, turning every 20 to 30 minutes to cook on all sides. Remove the sausage from the smoker and carefully remove the foil. Smoke the sausage without the foil for an additional 2 hours, turning the sausage every 20 minutes or so to smoke evenly.

When the sausage is done, you can eat it as is or use as directed in my recipes. The sausage can be refrigerated or frozen until ready to use.

PER ½ POUND	KCAL	FATgm	CHOLmg	SODmg
	340	2	189	120

TURKEY SAUSAGE WITH SPICY TOMATOES

MAKES 3 SERVINGS

THIS CAN BE served over rice or fettuccine.

1 *pound Smoked Turkey Sausage (page 110), cut into bite-size pieces*
1 *cup chopped onions*
½ *cup chopped green bell pepper*
1 *clove garlic, minced*
One *8-ounce can whole tomatoes*
3 *tablespoons tomato paste*

2 *teaspoons very finely chopped jalapeño peppers*
½ *teaspoon sugar*
½ *teaspoon chili powder*
¼ *teaspoon ground red pepper*
1½ *cups Chicken Stock (page 20) or water*

Spray the inside of a large pot with nonstick vegetable cooking spray and place over high heat. Add the sausage; cook, stirring, for 5 minutes, or until the sausage is browned. (If the sausage starts to stick to the bottom of the pot, remove from the heat and spray again with cooking spray, scraping the bottom of the pot well, then return to the heat.) Remove the sausage from the pot and set aside.

Remove the pot from the heat and spray the inside heavily with nonstick vegetable cooking spray. Add the onions, bell pepper and garlic; place over high heat and sauté for 5 minutes, stirring often. Reduce the heat to medium and stir in the remaining ingredients except for the stock. Cook for 10 minutes, stirring frequently. Add the stock and bring to a boil. Cover, reduce the heat and simmer for 20 minutes.

PER SERVING	KCAL	FATgm	CHOLmg	SODmg
	282	2	126	282

CHICKEN AND SAUSAGE JAMBALAYA

MAKES 6 SERVINGS

1 *pound skinned and boned chicken breasts, cut into bite-size pieces*
1 *pound Smoked Turkey Sausage (page 110), cut into bite-size pieces*
2 *medium tomatoes, peeled, seeded and chopped (about 1 cup)*
1 *cup finely chopped onions*
½ *cup finely chopped green bell pepper*
½ *cup finely chopped celery*

2½ *cups Chicken Stock (page 20) or water*
¼ *teaspoon salt*
¼ *teaspoon ground thyme*
¼ *teaspoon ground oregano*
¼ *teaspoon ground red pepper*
2 *cups hot cooked rice*
¼ *cup finely chopped green onions*
2 *tablespoons finely chopped fresh parsley*

Spray the inside of a large cast-iron pot with nonstick vegetable cooking spray. Place the skillet over high heat. When the skillet is very hot, add the chicken and sausage; cook, stirring constantly for 10 minutes, until browned. Add the tomatoes, onions, bell pepper and celery and cook for 15 minutes, stirring often.

Add the stock, salt, thyme, oregano and pepper; cover and simmer for 15 minutes, stirring often. Remove the skillet from the heat and stir in the rice, green onions and parsley. Cover and let stand for 5 minutes before serving.

PER SERVING	KCAL	FATgm	CHOLmg	SODmg
	321	3.5	127	193

STUFFED-ENOUGH TURKEY BREAST

MAKES 6 SERVINGS

½ teaspoon granulated sugar
½ teaspoon salt
½ teaspoon ground white pepper
½ teaspoon minced fresh garlic
½ teaspoon onion powder
½ teaspoon ground cumin
½ teaspoon gumbo filé
½ teaspoon ground red pepper
½ teaspoon paprika
½ teaspoon ground black pepper
1 tablespoon vegetable oil
2 cups finely chopped onions
1 cup finely chopped green bell pepper
½ cup finely chopped celery
1 large carrot, very finely shredded
1 large potato, peeled and very finely shredded
½ cup very finely chopped green onions
1½ pounds skinned and boned whole turkey breast, sliced in half lengthwise

Preheat the oven to 350°F.

In a small bowl, combine all the dry seasonings, mix well and set aside. Heat the vegetable oil in a medium skillet over high heat. Add the onions, bell pepper and celery; sauté, stirring for 10 minutes. Add the carrot, potato, green onions, and *half* the seasoning mix. Sauté, stirring for 10 minutes longer, then remove from the heat and set aside.

Sprinkle the turkey breast with the remaining seasoning mix. Spoon the cooked mixture along the center of one breast half; top with the remaining breast half and secure with cooking string. Place in a shallow baking dish that has been sprayed with nonstick vegetable cooking spray. Cover with aluminum foil and bake for 30 minutes. Uncover and bake for 15 minutes longer, or until the turkey is tender and golden brown.

PER SERVING	KCAL	FATgm	CHOLmg	SODmg
	217	2	95	264

SMOTHERED TURKEY WITH ONIONS

MAKES 4 SERVINGS

½ teaspoon salt
1 teaspoon ground red pepper
¼ teaspoon ground marjoram
1 pound skinned and boned turkey breast, cut into ½-inch strips
1 cup finely chopped onions
½ cup finely chopped green bell pepper

½ cup finely chopped celery
2 tablespoons salt-free chicken bouillon granules
2 cups water
1 teaspoon browning and seasoning sauce
2 cups hot cooked rice

Sprinkle the salt, pepper and marjoram over the turkey strips and mix well. Spray the inside of a large skillet with nonstick vegetable cooking spray and place over high heat. Add the turkey and cook for 15 minutes, stirring often to prevent burning.

Add the onions, bell pepper and celery; cover, and sauté for 15 minutes, stirring often and scraping the bottom of the skillet with a spoon. Reduce the heat to medium. Dissolve the bouillon in the water and add to the skillet along with the browning sauce. Cook, covered, for 15 minutes, or until the turkey is tender. Serve over rice.

PER SERVING	KCAL	FATgm	CHOLmg	SODmg
	266	1	95	336

MARINATED TURKEY AND GREEN PEPPERS

MAKES 4 SERVINGS

1 *pound skinned and boned turkey breast, cut into ½-inch strips*
2 *tablespoons low-sodium soy sauce*
1 *teaspoon minced fresh garlic*
1 *teaspoon ground red pepper*
1 *teaspoon ground ginger*
¼ *teaspoon salt*
½ *teaspoon dry hot mustard*
½ *teaspoon dried fennel seeds*

1 *medium green bell pepper, sliced into thin rings*
1 *cup finely chopped onions*
½ *cup finely chopped celery*
1 *teaspoon cornstarch*
1 *cup water*
2 *medium tomatoes, quartered*

In a large glass bowl, combine the turkey and the next 7 ingredients, mixing well. Cover and marinate overnight in the refrigerator.

The next day, spray the inside of a medium skillet with nonstick vegetable cooking spray and place over high heat. Add the turkey and cook for 10 minutes, stirring often. Add the bell pepper, onions and celery and cook for 10 minutes longer. Dissolve the cornstarch in the water and add to the skillet. Cook for an additional 15 minutes, or until the turkey is tender, stirring occasionally.

PER SERVING	KCAL	FATgm	CHOLmg	SODmg
	218	4	79	483

TURKEY PATTIES WITH SONNY SAUCE

MAKES 4 SERVINGS

1 *pound ground turkey*
1 *tablespoon minced fresh onion*
1 *teaspoon paprika*
¼ *teaspoon salt*
½ *teaspoon chili powder*
½ *teaspoon ground red pepper*
1 *cup finely chopped onions*
⅓ *cup finely chopped green bell pepper*
⅓ *cup finely chopped celery*
½ *teaspoon cornstarch*
1 *cup Chicken Stock (page 20) or water*
1 *teaspoon low-sodium Worcestershire sauce*
1 *teaspoon low-sodium soy sauce*
½ *teaspoon browning and seasoning sauce*

In a large bowl, combine the turkey and the next 5 ingredients. Mix well, then shape to form 4 patties, about 4 ounces each. Spray the inside of a medium skillet with nonstick vegetable cooking spray and place over high heat. Add the turkey patties and cook for 8 minutes, or until brown on both sides, turning often with a spatula. Remove the patties and keep warm.

Spray the skillet again with nonstick vegetable cooking spray and place over high heat. Add the onions, bell pepper and celery and sauté stirring, for 5 minutes. Dissolve the cornstarch in the stock and add to the skillet along with all the remaining ingredients. Cook for 10 minutes, or until the sauce thickens. Place the patties on individual plates. Spoon the sauce over each patty and serve hot.

PER SERVING	KCAL	FATgm	CHOLmg	SODmg
	99	4	79	288

PORCUPINE MEATBALLS

MAKES 6 SERVINGS

*J*MY NEIGHBOR came over for coffee one day and gave me her recipe for Porcupine Meatballs. She said, "This one is tailor-made for busy moms like you." Her original version is made with ground beef and cream, but I changed some of the ingredients for a low-calorie dish.

1 *pound ground turkey*
  breast
One *10½-ounce can*
  reduced-calorie cream
  of mushroom soup
1 *cup quick-cooking (not*
  instant) rice
½ *cup dehydrated onion*
⅓ *cup finely chopped*
  green onions
½ *teaspoon salt*

½ *teaspoon granulated*
  garlic
½ *teaspoon dried basil*
  leaves, crushed
¼ *teaspoon ground white*
  pepper
⅛ *teaspoon ground black*
  pepper
⅓ *cup tomato paste*
½ *cup Chicken Stock*
  (page 20) or water

Preheat the oven to 350°F.

In a large bowl, combine all the ingredients except for the tomato paste and stock. To make the mixture easier to work with, spray your clean, dry hands with nonstick vegetable cooking spray and mix the ingredients well.

Place about 2 tablespoons of the mixture in the palm of your hand and roll it into a ball, pressing firmly enough so that it stays together. Arrange the meatballs close together in an 8-inch-square baking dish that has been sprayed with nonstick vegetable cooking spray. Dissolve the tomato paste in the stock and pour over the meatballs. Cover with aluminum foil and bake for 1 hour, or until the rice is tender.

PER SERVING	KCAL	FATgm	CHOLmg	SODmg
	243	1	63	390

TURKEY-EGGPLANT CASSEROLE

MAKES 6 SERVINGS

2 tablespoons reduced-calorie margarine
1 pound ground turkey
2 large eggplants, peeled and cubed (about 8 cups)
1 tablespoon low-sodium Worcestershire sauce
2 teaspoons minced fresh garlic
½ teaspoon salt
1 teaspoon ground white pepper

2 cups Chicken Stock (page 20) or water
3 slices bread (40 calories per slice), cut into ½-inch cubes
½ cup finely chopped green onions
Two ¾-ounce slices reduced-fat American-cheese product, cut into ½-inch strips

Preheat the oven to 350°F.

In a large pot over high heat, heat the margarine until very hot. Add the turkey and sauté for 10 minutes, stirring often. Add the next 5 ingredients; sauté, stirring, for 10 minutes more. Add the stock and cook for 5 more minutes, stirring often. Remove from the heat and stir in the bread cubes and green onions; set aside.

Spray the inside of an 8-inch-square baking dish with nonstick vegetable cooking spray. Spoon in the eggplant mixture and top with the cheese. Bake for 15 minutes.

PER SERVING	KCAL	FATgm	CHOLmg	SODmg
	225	4	52	255

TURKEY WITH SPANISH RICE

MAKES 3 SERVINGS

2   *slices lean bacon*
½   *cup finely chopped onions*
¼   *cup finely chopped green bell pepper*
¼   *cup finely chopped celery*
1¼ *cups Chicken Stock (page 20) or water*

1   *cup chopped cooked turkey*
¼ *cup uncooked rice*
⅓ *cup finely chopped green onions*
3   *tablespoons tomato paste*
¼ *teaspoon ground white pepper*

In a medium saucepan over high heat, fry the bacon until very crisp, turning often. Drain the bacon on paper towels and crumble; discard the grease. Combine the bacon, onions, bell pepper and celery in the saucepan and place over medium heat. Sauté for 10 minutes, stirring often. Reduce the heat to low and stir in all the remaining ingredients. Cover and cook for 30 minutes, or until the rice is tender, stirring occasionally.

PER SERVING	KCAL	FATgm	CHOLmg	SODmg
	201	6	43	129

TURKEY DINNER IN A BAG

MAKES 4 SERVINGS

J WHEN MY KIDS were growing up and participating in sports and after-school activities, I made this dish frequently. Sonny was on the football team, Annette was a cheerleader and Toni was a flag girl, so we were always going to or coming from practice. What I liked best about this dish was how easy it was (and is) to prepare; when we returned home, our dinner was ready.

2 *tablespoons minced fresh onion*
½ *teaspoon salt*
½ *teaspoon chili powder*
½ *teaspoon ground white pepper*
1 *pound boneless turkey breast*

1 *pound whole fresh green beans*
2 *medium potatoes, peeled and chopped (about 1 cup)*
2 *medium turnips, peeled and chopped (about 1 cup)*

Preheat the oven to 350°F.

In a small bowl, combine the onion, salt, chili powder and white pepper; mix well and set aside. Place the turkey, green beans, potatoes and turnips in a 10-by-16-inch oven cooking bag; sprinkle with the seasoning mixture, seal the bag and shake to distribute the seasoning. Place the bag in a shallow baking dish and bake for 2 hours, or until the turkey is very tender.

PER SERVING	KCAL	FATgm	CHOLmg	SODmg
	280	1.3	97	343

CHRIS'S TURKEY STROGANOFF

MAKES 4 SERVINGS

*J*MY SON-IN-LAW CHRIS ONCALE is one of my chefs at our restaurant. His favorite dish is beef Stroganoff, which he prepares very well. I substituted turkey and it still tastes great!

1 *pound boneless turkey breast*
1 *cup thinly sliced fresh mushrooms*
1 *cup finely chopped onions*
⅓ *cup dry sherry*
¼ *teaspoon salt*
⅛ *teaspoon ground white pepper*

⅛ *teaspoon ground red pepper*
2 *teaspoons cornstarch*
2¼ *cups Chicken Stock (page 20) or water*
1 *cup low-fat cottage cheese*
1 *tablespoon lemon juice*
2 *teaspoons finely chopped fresh parsley*

Preheat a coal or gas grill.

Grill the turkey breast over hot coals or on a griddle for about 5 minutes per side, or until brown. Let cool, then cut into 1-inch strips and set aside.

Spray the inside of a medium skillet with nonstick vegetable cooking spray and place over high heat. Add the mushrooms and onions and sauté for 1 minute, stirring often. Add the sherry, salt and white and red peppers; boil for 1 minute, or until the liquid is reduced to half.

Dissolve the cornstarch in ¼ cup of the stock; slowly stir into the vegetable mixture along with the remaining 2 cups stock. Continue cooking and stirring for 5 minutes, or until the sauce is thickened.

Place the cottage cheese in a blender and process until smooth. Add to skillet along with the turkey, lemon juice and parsley. Reduce the heat and simmer for 10 minutes, or until the turkey is done.

PER SERVING	KCAL	FATgm	CHOLmg	SODmg
	228	1.6	97	416

TURKEY CURRY

MAKES 6 SERVINGS

1   *pound skinned and boned turkey dark meat, cut into bite-size pieces*
1½ *teaspoons ground curry*
1½ *teaspoons ground ginger*
½   *teaspoon salt*
½   *teaspoon ground red pepper*
½   *teaspoon ground coriander*
1   *cup finely chopped onions*
½ *cup finely chopped celery*
2 *cups Chicken Stock (page 20) or water*
2 *medium apples, chopped (about 2 cups)*
½ *cup raisins*
1 *tablespoon honey*
1 *teaspoon balsamic vinegar*
2 *teaspoons cornstarch*
2 *cups cooked rice*

Spray the inside of a large skillet with nonstick vegetable cooking spray and place over high heat. Add the turkey and sauté, stirring for 10 minutes. Combine the next 5 ingredients in a small bowl; mix well and sprinkle over the turkey. Add the onions and celery; cover, and cook for 10 minutes more, stirring often.

Add *1 cup* of the stock and continue to cook, covered, for 10 minutes. Add the apples, raisins, honey and vinegar; cook for 15 minutes more.

Dissolve the cornstarch in the remaining stock and add to the skillet. Cook, uncovered, for 10 minutes, or until the sauce thickens, stirring often. Reduce the heat to simmer and stir in the rice. Cook for 5 minutes, stirring often. Remove from the heat and let stand a few minutes before serving.

PER SERVING	KCAL	FATgm	CHOLmg	SODmg
	291	6	64	238

1-2-3 CASSEROLE

MAKES 6 SERVINGS

1 **pound ground turkey breast**
2 **cups Chicken Stock (page 20) or water**
1 **cup finely chopped onions**
½ **cup finely chopped green bell pepper**
½ **cup finely chopped celery**
1 **teaspoon salt**
1 **teaspoon granulated garlic**

1 **teaspoon browning and seasoning sauce**
½ **teaspoon ground red pepper**
1 **quart water**
2 **medium eggplants, peeled and chopped (about 8 cups)**
1 **cup whole Corn Chex**
½ **cup crumbled Corn Chex**
1 **tablespoon grated Parmesan cheese**

Preheat the oven to 350°F.

Spray the inside of a medium skillet with nonstick vegetable cooking spray and place over high heat. Add the turkey and sauté for 10 minutes, or until brown, stirring often. Add next 8 ingredients; cook 15 minutes longer, stirring occasionally.

In a large saucepan over high heat, bring the water to a boil. Add the eggplant and boil for 10 minutes; drain and set aside.

Spray the inside of an 8-inch-square baking dish with nonstick vegetable cooking spray. Arrange *half* the eggplant on the bottom, then layer with *half* the turkey, then *half* the whole Corn Chex. Repeat with remaining ingredients, then top with crumbled Chex and sprinkle with the cheese. Bake for 30 minutes.

PER SERVING	KCAL	FATgm	CHOLmg	SODmg
	185	1.3	64	468

TURKEY-CABBAGE ROLLS

MAKES 6 SERVINGS

5 *cups water*
6 *large cabbage leaves*
1 *pound ground turkey*
1 *teaspoon salt*
½ *teaspoon ground thyme*
½ *teaspoon paprika*
¼ *teaspoon ground red*
   pepper
¼ *teaspoon ground black*
   pepper
3 *cups shredded cabbage*
1 *cup finely chopped*
   onions

½ *cup finely chopped*
   green bell pepper
½ *cup finely chopped*
   celery
⅓ *cup finely chopped*
   green onions
¾ *cup tomato paste, in all*
3 *cups Chicken Stock*
   (page 20) or water

Preheat the oven to 350°F.

In a large saucepan over high heat, bring the water to a boil. Place the cabbage leaves in the boiling water; cover, and cook for 5 minutes. Reduce the heat and simmer, uncovered, for 5 minutes. Drain the cabbage and set aside until cool to the touch.

Spray the same saucepan with nonstick vegetable cooking spray and place over high heat. Add the turkey and all the dry seasonings; sauté, stirring for 10 minutes, or until brown. Add the shredded cabbage, onions, bell pepper, celery and green onions; sauté, stirring, for 10 minutes longer. Dissolve *half* the tomato paste in *1 cup* of the stock. Add to the saucepan and cook for 5 minutes.

Place the cabbage leaves on a clean, flat surface. Spoon about ½ cup of the meat mixture across the center of each leaf.

Carefully fold in thirds and place seam side down in an 8-inch-square baking dish that has been sprayed with nonstick vegetable cooking spray. Dissolve the remaining tomato paste in the remaining 2 cups stock and spoon over the cabbage rolls. Cover with aluminum foil and bake for 1 hour.

PER SERVING	KCAL	FATgm	CHOLmg	SODmg
	157	1	58	471

TURKEY LOAF SUPREME

MAKES 4 SERVINGS

½ *pound ground turkey*
½ *cup very finely chopped*
    onions
¼ *cup very finely chopped*
    green bell pepper
2 *slices bread (40 calories*
    per slice), toasted
    and finely crumbled
1 *medium egg, beaten*
    well

¼ *cup evaporated skim*
    milk
1 *tablespoon low-sodium*
    Worcestershire sauce
¼ *teaspoon salt*
⅛ *teaspoon ground black*
    pepper

Preheat the oven to 350°F.

In a large bowl, combine all the ingredients; mix well. Shape the mixture into a loaf and place in a 9-by-5-inch glass loaf pan that has been sprayed with nonstick vegetable cooking spray. Cover with aluminum foil and bake for 1 hour.

PER SERVING	KCAL	FATgm	CHOLmg	SODmg
	143	2	116	202

SOUTHERN-STYLE OVEN-FRIED CHICKEN

MAKES 4 SERVINGS

*T*RADITIONAL southern fried chicken was deep-fried in oil, but by baking it in the oven you can achieve the same crisp, crunchy texture as fried.

One 2½-to-3-pound chicken
¼ teaspoon salt
½ teaspoon granulated garlic
¼ teaspoon curry powder
¼ teaspoon ground cumin
¼ teaspoon ground oregano
¼ teaspoon paprika
¼ teaspoon ground red pepper

¼ teaspoon ground black pepper
½ cup all-purpose flour
¼ cup yellow cornmeal
½ cup buttermilk
1 tablespoon low-sodium Worcestershire sauce
1 tablespoon prepared mustard

Preheat the oven to 350°F.

Remove the skin and fat from chicken and discard. Cut the chicken into serving-size pieces, then debone the breast. (Reserve the wings, back and bones from the breast to use for stock.)

In a small bowl, combine the next 8 ingredients. Mix well and reserve ½ teaspoon of the seasoning mix; sprinkle the remaining seasoning over the chicken and set aside.

In a shallow baking dish, combine the flour, cornmeal, and the reserved seasoning; mix well and set aside.

In a medium bowl, beat together the milk, Worcestershire, and mustard. Add the chicken and coat well, then dredge in the flour mixture. Arrange the chicken pieces on a large baking sheet that has been sprayed with butter-flavored nonstick vegetable cooking spray. Spray each piece of chicken with the nonstick vegetable cooking spray; this keeps the moisture in. Bake for 30 minutes, or until golden brown and crisp tender.

PER SERVING	KCAL	FATgm	CHOLmg	SODmg
	353	10	130	304

OVEN-BARBECUED CHICKEN A LA TAMMY

MAKES 4 SERVINGS

1 teaspoon ground
   marjoram
½ teaspoon paprika
¼ teaspoon salt
¼ teaspoon granulated
   garlic
⅛ teaspoon ground white
   pepper
⅛ teaspoon ground red
   pepper
⅛ teaspoon ground black
   pepper
2 chicken thighs, skin
   and fat removed
2 chicken legs, skin and
   fat removed

1 cup very finely chopped
   onions
½ cup very finely chopped
   green bell pepper
2 cups Chicken Stock
   (page 20) or water
¼ cup tomato paste
1 tablespoon low-sodium
   Worcestershire sauce
1 teaspoon Dijon mustard
½ teaspoon brown sugar
   substitute
½ teaspoon lemon juice
¼ teaspoon liquid smoke
¼ teaspoon salt

Preheat the oven to 350°F.

In a small bowl, combine the first 7 ingredients and mix well. Sprinkle *half* the seasoning over both sides of the chicken and place the pieces in a baking dish that has been sprayed with nonstick vegetable cooking spray; set aside.

Spray the inside of a large skillet with nonstick vegetable cooking spray and place over medium heat. Add the onions and bell pepper; sauté, stirring, for 1 minute. Add the remaining seasoning mix and all the remaining ingredients. Cook for 15 minutes, stirring often. Remove from the heat; baste the chicken with sauce and bake for 20 minutes, or until tender, basting the chicken often.

PER SERVING	KCAL	FATgm	CHOLmg	SODmg
	181	7	69	219

BLACKENED CHICKEN BREAST

MAKES 1 SERVING

THE BLACKENING PROCESS gives this chicken a very special flavor. Served with a baked potato and salad, it can't be beat!

½ *teaspoon paprika*
⅛ *teaspoon salt*
¼ *teaspoon ground red
   pepper*
¼ *teaspoon ground cumin*
¼ *teaspoon ground thyme*

⅛ *teaspoon ground white
   pepper*
⅛ *teaspoon onion powder*
1 *boneless chicken breast
   half, skinned*

Preheat the oven to 350°F.

Heat a medium cast-iron skillet over high heat for 15 minutes, or until very hot. In a small bowl, combine all the dry seasonings; mix well and set aside.

Spray one side of the chicken with nonstick vegetable cooking spray and sprinkle with *half* the seasoning; reserve the remaining seasoning. Place in the very hot skillet, seasoned side down. Repeat procedure with top side of the chicken; cook for 1 minute on each side.

Remove from the skillet and place on a small baking sheet that has been sprayed with nonstick vegetable cooking spray. Bake for 5 minutes.

PER SERVING	KCAL	FATgm	CHOLmg	SODmg
	243	5	120	350

CHICKEN SAUCE PIQUANT

MAKES 4 SERVINGS

IN CAJUN FRENCH *piquant* means "thorn," like the thorn from a rosebush. The pepper in this sauce piquant stings the palate!

1 *tablespoon olive oil*
4 *whole chicken breasts, skinned and boned*
2 *large onions, finely chopped*
¼ *cup finely chopped celery*
¼ *cup finely chopped green bell pepper*
2 *cloves garlic, minced*
3 *tablespoons all-purpose flour*
One 6-*ounce can low-sodium tomato sauce*

2 *medium tomatoes, peeled, seeded and chopped (about 1 cup)*
⅛ *teaspoon dried basil leaves, crushed*
⅛ *teaspoon ground red pepper*
⅛ *teaspoon ground black pepper*
¼ *cup finely chopped green onions*
3 *tablespoons very finely chopped fresh parsley*
2 *cups hot cooked rice*

In a large heavy skillet over medium heat, heat the olive oil. Add the chicken and brown it on both sides. Remove the chicken and set aside. Add the onions, celery, bell pepper and garlic to the skillet and sauté for 15 minutes, stirring often. Stir in the flour and cook for 10 minutes, or until brown, stirring constantly. Add the tomato sauce, tomatoes, basil and red and black peppers. Reduce the heat and simmer, covered, for 15 minutes, stirring occasionally.

Add the chicken, cover and continue cooking for 30 minutes, or until the chicken is tender. Add the green onions and parsley and cook for 1 minute. Serve over rice.

PER SERVING	KCAL	FATgm	CHOLmg	SODmg
	418	7	120	133

CHICKEN AND SPAGHETTI

MAKES 5 SERVINGS

IN CAJUN COUNTRY we eat a lot of pasta! Everyone's favorite is chicken and spaghetti.

5 *boneless chicken breast halves (3 ounces each), cut into 1-inch strips*
1 *teaspoon salt*
½ *teaspoon ground black pepper*
⅓ *cup tomato paste*
1 *quart water*
1 *cup finely chopped onions*
½ *cup finely chopped green bell pepper*
½ *cup finely chopped celery*

1 *medium tomato, peeled, seeded and chopped (about ½ cup)*
½ *teaspoon dried basil leaves, crushed*
½ *teaspoon ground oregano*
½ *teaspoon ground thyme*
½ *teaspoon ground marjoram*
One 8-ounce package *spaghetti*

Spray a large saucepan with nonstick vegetable cooking spray and place over high heat. Add the chicken and sprinkle with the salt and pepper. Cook for 10 minutes, or until brown on both sides, stirring frequently.

Dissolve the tomato paste in *1 cup* of the water; add to the saucepan along with the onions, bell pepper and celery. Cook, stirring, for 10 minutes. Stir in the remaining *3 cups* water and the remaining ingredients. Reduce the heat to medium; cover and simmer for 25 minutes, stirring frequently.

Meanwhile cook the spaghetti according to package directions, omitting the salt; drain and set aside.

Remove the saucepan from the heat. Add the spaghetti and stir until thoroughly mixed. Cover and let stand for 5 minutes before serving.

PER SERVING	KCAL	FATgm	CHOLmg	SODmg
	252	3.75	75	291

CHICKEN FETTUCCINE

MAKES 3 SERVINGS

1 *cup low-fat cottage cheese*

2 *skinned and boned chicken breast halves (about 5 ounces each), cut into ½-inch strips*

1 *cup thinly sliced fresh mushrooms*

½ *cup finely chopped green onions*

¼ *teaspoon salt*

½ *teaspoon granulated garlic*

½ *teaspoon dried basil leaves, crushed*

⅛ *teaspoon ground white pepper*

⅛ *teaspoon ground red pepper*

⅛ *teaspoon ground oregano*

½ *cup Chicken Stock (page 20) or water*

1 *cup evaporated skim milk*

1½ *cups cooked fettuccine*

Place the cottage cheese in a blender and process until smooth; set aside.

Spray the inside of a medium skillet with nonstick vegetable cooking spray and place over high heat. Add the chicken and sauté, stirring, for 5 minutes. Add the mushrooms, green onions, and all the dry seasonings; cook, stirring, for 5 minutes. Add the stock and cook for 2 minutes, stirring often.

Add the milk and ⅓ cup of the blended cottage cheese to the skillet (refrigerate remaining cottage cheese for another use). Cook, stirring for 3 minutes, or until the sauce begins to thicken, then add fettuccine and continue cooking until the sauce is the desired thickness.

PER SERVING	KCAL	FATgm	CHOLmg	SODmg
	356	5	85	486

CHICKEN POT PIE

MAKES 6 SERVINGS

THIS IS A good way to use leftover chicken.

½ *teaspoon salt*
½ *teaspoon chili powder*
½ *teaspoon paprika*
¼ *teaspoon ground red pepper*
⅛ *teaspoon ground marjoram*

⅛ *teaspoon ground sage*
3 *cups chopped cooked chicken*
1 *egg plus 2 egg whites*
1 *cup evaporated skim milk*
1 *cup quick-mixing flour*

Preheat the oven to 375°F.

In a small bowl, combine ¼ teaspoon of the salt and all of the chili powder, paprika, red pepper, marjoram and sage; mix well and sprinkle over chicken; set aside.

In a medium bowl, beat together the egg, egg whites, milk, and remaining salt. Gradually add the flour, mixing well.

Spray the inside of a 9-inch pie pan with nonstick vegetable cooking spray. Pour in half of the batter; arrange the chicken over the batter, then top with the remaining batter. Bake for 30 minutes, or until golden brown.

PER SERVING	KCAL	FATgm	CHOLmg	SODmg
	238	6	109	300

CHICKEN CROQUETTES

MAKES 4 SERVINGS

A SOUTHERN favorite.

1 tablespoon reduced-
    calorie margarine
½ cup finely chopped
    onions
¼ cup finely chopped green
    onions
¼ cup finely chopped celery
2 teaspoons quick-mixing
    flour
½ cup Chicken Stock (page
    20) or water

¼ cup frozen egg
    substitute, thawed
2 cups finely chopped
    cooked chicken
⅛ teaspoon salt
⅛ teaspoon ground sage
⅛ teaspoon ground
    oregano
⅛ teaspoon ground red
    pepper
⅓ cup dry sherry
1 cup crushed whole
    wheat crackers

In a large saucepan over medium heat, melt the margarine. Add the onions, green onions and celery; cook for 5 minutes, stirring often. Add the flour and cook for 1 minute longer, stirring constantly. Add the stock, reduce the heat and simmer for about 5 minutes, or until the mixture thickens. Slowly stir in the egg substitute, then add the chicken and seasonings; cook for 10 minutes, stirring often. Remove from the heat and stir in the sherry. Let the mixture cool slightly, then refrigerate for at least 1 hour.

Preheat the oven to 375°F.

When the mixture is well chilled, shape it into 1½-inch balls and roll them in the crushed crackers. Arrange the croquettes 1 inch apart on a baking sheet that has been sprayed with nonstick vegetable cooking spray. Bake for 15 minutes, then increase the temperature to 400°F and bake for 15 minutes longer.

PER SERVING	KCAL	FATgm	CHOLmg	SODmg
	218	9	47	155

SAUTEED CHICKEN AND MUSHROOMS

MAKES 3 SERVINGS

1   *teaspoon granulated garlic*
½   *teaspoon paprika*
¼   *teaspoon salt*
¼   *teaspoon ground white pepper*
¼   *teaspoon ground thyme*
2   *boneless chicken breast halves (about 5 ounces each), skinned and cut into 1-inch strips*

1   *tablespoon cornstarch*
1½ *cups Chicken Stock (page 20) or water*
1   *cup thinly sliced fresh mushrooms*
½   *cup finely chopped green onions*
1   *tablespoon dehydrated onion*
⅛   *teaspoon browning and seasoning sauce*

In a small bowl, combine the garlic, paprika, salt, white pepper and thyme; mix well and sprinkle over the chicken. Spray the inside of a large skillet with nonstick vegetable cooking spray and place over high heat. Add the chicken and sauté for 10 minutes, stirring often and scraping the bottom of the skillet with a wooden spoon. (If chicken starts to stick, remove the skillet from the heat and spray again with nonstick vegetable cooking spray; return to the heat.)

Dissolve the cornstarch in *1* cup of the stock and add it to the mixture. Stir in the mushrooms, green onions, dehydrated onion, browning sauce and the remaining ½ cup stock. Reduce the heat, cover and simmer for 30 minutes, stirring often.

PER SERVING	KCAL	FATgm	CHOLmg	SODmg
	183	4	80	238

CHICKEN À LA KING

MAKES 4 SERVINGS

2 *tablespoons reduced-calorie margarine*
1 *cup thinly sliced fresh mushrooms*
½ *cup finely chopped onions*
¼ *cup finely chopped green bell pepper*
2 *tablespoons finely chopped red bell pepper*

1 *tablespoon cornstarch*
2 *cups evaporated skim milk*
2 *cups chopped cooked chicken*
¼ *teaspoon salt*
½ *teaspoon ground white pepper*
⅛ *teaspoon ground red pepper*

In a large saucepan over high heat, melt the margarine. Add the mushrooms, onions and green and red bell peppers; sauté for 10 minutes, stirring often.

Dissolve the cornstarch in a small amount of the milk; add to the saucepan along with the remaining milk; cook, stirring constantly, for about 2 minutes, or until sauce thickens. Add all the remaining ingredients and cook for 5 minutes more, stirring often.

PER SERVING	KCAL	FATgm	CHOLmg	SODmg
	178	8	65	252

CHICKEN YA-YA

MAKES 4 SERVINGS

WHEN THIS DISH came out of the oven and everyone was sampling it, someone yelled, "Oh, oh! Ya, ya!" And so it was named.

One 2½- to 3-pound chicken, skinned and halved
½ teaspoon salt
½ teaspoon ground red pepper
½ teaspoon chili powder
½ teaspoon paprika
1 tablespoon reduced-calorie margarine
1 cup finely chopped onions
½ cup finely chopped green bell pepper

½ cup finely chopped celery
One 6-ounce can unsweetened orange juice
2 tablespoons tomato paste
2 tablespoons honey
1 tablespoon low-sodium Worcestershire sauce
1 teaspoon grated orange peel
¼ teaspoon ground ginger
¼ teaspoon hot pepper sauce

Preheat the oven to 350°F.

Arrange the chicken halves in an 8-inch-square baking dish that has been sprayed with nonstick vegetable cooking spray. Combine the salt, red pepper, chili powder and paprika; mix well and sprinkle over the chicken; set aside.

In a medium skillet over high heat, melt the margarine. Add the onions, bell pepper and celery; sauté, stirring, for 5 minutes. Add all the remaining ingredients. Cook, stirring, for 5 minutes longer, or until the sauce thickens, then remove from the heat and pour over the chicken.

Cover with aluminum foil and bake for 30 minutes. Turn the chicken over and baste with the sauce. Bake, uncovered, for 30 minutes longer, or until the chicken is tender, basting often.

PER SERVING	KCAL	FATgm	CHOLmg	SODmg
	188	12	129	450

ROSEMARY AND GINGER CHICKEN

MAKES 4 SERVINGS

½ *teaspoon salt*
1 *teaspoon ground red pepper*
One *1½-to-2-pound whole chicken, skin and fat removed*
2 *cups coarsely chopped onions*
¼ *cup coarsely chopped green bell pepper*

1 *tablespoon whole rosemary*
2 *teaspoons peeled and grated ginger*
3 *tablespoons water*
1 *tablespoon browning and seasoning sauce*

Preheat the oven to 350°F.

Mix the salt and red pepper together and sprinkle *half* over the chicken and inside the cavity; reserve the remaining seasoning.

In a medium bowl, combine the onions, bell pepper, rosemary, ginger and the remaining seasoning; spray heavily with nonstick vegetable cooking spray and mix well. Stuff the mixture inside the chicken cavity and set aside.

Spray the inside of an 8-inch-square baking dish with nonstick vegetable cooking spray. Place the chicken in a dish and spray again with the cooking spray. Cover with aluminum foil and bake for 1 hour. Remove from the oven and uncover. Mix the water and browning sauce together and use it to baste the chicken thoroughly. Return the chicken to the oven and bake, uncovered, for 20 minutes longer. Remove the chicken from the oven and let cool for 15 minutes. Remove the stuffing mixture and discard before serving.

PER SERVING	KCAL	FATgm	CHOLmg	SODmg
	299	12	14	260

GINGER-AND-OREGANO-STUFFED CHICKEN

MAKES 4 SERVINGS

½ *teaspoon salt*
1 *teaspoon ground red pepper*
One *1½-to-2-pound whole chicken, skin and fat removed*
2 *cups coarsely chopped onions*
¼ *cup coarsely chopped green bell pepper*

2 *tablespoons whole oregano*
2 *teaspoons peeled and grated ginger*
3 *tablespoons water*
1 *tablespoon browning and seasoning sauce*

Preheat the oven to 350°F.

Mix the salt and red pepper together and sprinkle *half* over the chicken and inside the cavity; reserve the remaining seasoning.

In a medium bowl, combine the onions, bell pepper, oregano, ginger and the remaining seasoning; spray heavily with nonstick vegetable cooking spray and mix well. Stuff the mixture inside the chicken cavity and set aside.

Spray the inside of an 8-inch-square baking dish with nonstick vegetable cooking spray. Place the chicken in the dish and spray again with the cooking spray. Cover with aluminum foil and bake for 1 hour. Remove from the oven and uncover. Mix the water and browning sauce together and use it to baste the chicken thoroughly. Return the chicken to the oven and bake, uncovered, for 20 minutes longer. Remove the chicken from the oven and let cool for 15 minutes. Remove the stuffing mixture and discard before serving.

PER SERVING	KCAL	FATgm	CHOLmg	SODmg
	280	10	14	265

BAKED CHICKEN WITH BELINDA SAUCE

MAKES 4 SERVINGS

2 *cups Chicken Stock (page 20) or water*
One *¼-ounce envelope dried onion-mushroom soup mix*
1 *cup dry sherry*
½ *cup very finely chopped green onions*

4 *chicken quarters, skin and fat removed*
½ *teaspoon ground white pepper*
½ *teaspoon ground red pepper*

Preheat the oven to 350°F.

In a medium saucepan over high heat, bring the stock to a boil. Reduce the heat to medium and stir in the soup mix, sherry and green onions. Cook for 5 minutes, stirring often. Remove from the heat and set aside.

Sprinkle the white and red pepper over both sides of the chicken. Place in an 8- or 9-inch-square baking dish that has been sprayed with nonstick vegetable cooking spray. Pour the sauce over the chicken and bake, uncovered, for 30 minutes, or until the chicken is tender.

PER SERVING	KCAL	FATgm	CHOLmg	SODmg
	277	10	130	281

CHICKEN A LA HOWARD

MAKES 3 SERVINGS

2 *boneless chicken breast halves (about 5 ounces each), skinned and cut into ½-inch strips*

3 *medium tomatoes, peeled, seeded and pureed (1½ cups)*

2 *tablespoons chili powder*

1 *tablespoon dehydrated onion*

¼ *teaspoon salt*

¼ *teaspoon ground white pepper*

¼ *teaspoon ground cumin*

¼ *teaspoon ground oregano*

1 *cup Chicken Stock (page 20) or water*

Spray the inside of a large saucepan with nonstick vegetable cooking spray and place over medium heat. Add the chicken and cook for 15 minutes, or until brown on all sides, stirring often. Add all the remaining ingredients except for the stock: cook for 5 minutes more. Stir in the stock and cook for an additional 5 minutes, or until the sauce thickens.

PER SERVING	KCAL	FATgm	CHOLmg	SODmg
	191	4	80	271

FLORENTINE-STUFFED CHICKEN BREAST

MAKES 4 SERVINGS

ELEGANT ENOUGH to serve at your next dinner party.

4 *whole chicken breasts, skinned and boned*
1 *teaspoon salt-free lemon-pepper seasoning*
One *10-ounce package frozen chopped spinach*
1 *teaspoon reduced-calorie margarine*
1 *cup finely chopped onions*
½ *cup finely chopped green bell pepper*
⅛ *teaspoon salt*
⅛ *teaspoon granulated garlic*
⅛ *teaspoon ground white pepper*

⅛ *teaspoon ground oregano*
1 *tablespoon salt-free chicken bouillon granules*
¼ *cup hot water*
1 *teaspoon cider vinegar*
2 *slices bread (40 calories per slice), cut into ½-inch cubes*
2 *tablespoons freshly grated low-fat Parmesan cheese*
2 *tablespoons reduced-calorie mayonnaise*

Preheat the oven to 350°F.

Place the chicken breasts on a clean surface and pound them evenly with a mallet to a ⅛-inch thickness. Sprinkle the lemon-pepper seasoning on both sides of the chicken and set aside. Cook the spinach according to package directions, omitting the salt; drain and set aside.

In a medium saucepan over medium heat, melt the margarine. Add the onions, bell pepper, salt, white pepper and oregano; cook for 5 minutes, stirring often. Dissolve the bouillon granules in the hot water and add to the saucepan along with the spinach and vinegar.

Reduce the heat and simmer for 5 minutes. Add the bread cubes and cheese; cook, stirring for 1 minute more. Remove from the heat and stir in the mayonnaise. Spoon about 1½ tablespoons of the spinach mixture into the center of each chicken breast. Carefully fold the chicken around the mixture and place seam side down in a 9-by-5-by-3-inch loaf pan that has been heavily sprayed with nonstick vegetable cooking spray. Cover with aluminum foil and bake for 30 minutes; uncover and bake for an additional 30 minutes.

PER SERVING	KCAL	FATgm	CHOLmg	SODmg
	344	10	127	198

ENOLA'S CHICKEN SALAD

MAKES 1½ CUPS

1 *quart water*
2 *chicken quarters (thighs and legs), skinned*
2 *tablespoons reduced-calorie mayonnaise*
2 *tablespoons very finely chopped onions*
2 *tablespoons sweet pickle relish*

1 *tablespoon very finely chopped celery*
¼ *teaspoon salt*
⅛ *teaspoon ground white pepper*
⅛ *teaspoon ground black pepper*

In a large saucepan, bring the water and the chicken to a boil. Boil for 30 minutes, or until the chicken is tender. Drain, reserving the stock. When cool to the touch, remove the chicken from the bone and chop finely.

In a medium bowl, combine the chopped chicken and *1 table-spoon* of the reserved stock. Stir in all the remaining ingredients; mix well. Let stand for a few minutes before serving. (Refrigerate the remaining stock for another use.)

PER TABLESPOON	KCAL	FATgm	CHOLmg	SODmg
	21	1	8	60

HEN FRICASSEE A LA RUSSELL

MAKES 4 SERVINGS

One 1-to-1½-pound
   Cornish game hen,
   skinned and quartered
1 cup finely chopped
   onions
½ cup finely chopped
   green bell pepper
½ teaspoon salt
½ teaspoon ground white
   pepper
¼ teaspoon ground
   oregano

¼ teaspoon ground red
   pepper
2 tablespoons salt-free
   chicken bouillon
   granules
3 cups Chicken Stock
   (page 20) or water
3 tablespoons Roux Flour
   (page 18)
½ cup finely chopped
   green onions
2 cups hot cooked rice

Spray the inside of a large saucepan with nonstick vegetable cooking spray and place over high heat. Add the hen and cook for 10 minutes, or until brown on all sides, turning often. Add the next 6 ingredients; cook, stirring for 5 minutes. Dissolve the bouillon in the stock and add to the saucepan along with the roux flour, stirring well.

Reduce the heat, cover, and simmer for 25 minutes, stirring occasionally. Add the green onions and cook for 5 minutes more. Serve with hot rice.

PER SERVING	KCAL	FATgm	CHOLmg	SODmg
	286	5	66	315

CORNISH HEN WITH OYSTER STUFFING

MAKES 4 SERVINGS

One 1-to-1½-pound
    Cornish game hen, skin
    and fat removed
1 teaspoon paprika
¼ teaspoon salt
½ teaspoon granulated
    garlic
½ teaspoon dry hot
    mustard
½ teaspoon ground red
    pepper
1 tablespoon reduced-
    calorie margarine
1 cup finely chopped
    onions
½ cup finely chopped
    green bell pepper
½ cup finely chopped
    celery

1½ cups Chicken Stock
    (page 20) or water
½ cup oysters, drained
    and cut into bite-size
    pieces
1 cup Jalapeño
    Cornbread (page
    233), crumbled
1 slice bread (40 calories
    per slice), cut into
    ¼-inch cubes
1 egg
⅓ cup evaporated skim
    milk
¼ cup finely chopped
    green onions
⅛ cup very finely
    chopped fresh
    parsley

Preheat the oven to 375°F.

Wash the hen and pat dry; set aside. In a small bowl, mix together all the dry seasonings. Sprinkle *half* the seasoning mix over the hen; reserve the remaining seasoning. Set aside.

In a medium skillet over high heat, melt the margarine. Add the onions, bell pepper and celery and sauté, stirring for 10 minutes.

Add the stock and cook for 10 minutes, stirring often. Reduce the heat to simmer; add the chopped oysters, cornbread, bread cubes and the remaining seasoning mix. Beat together the egg and milk and slowly add to mixture, stirring constantly. Stir in

the green onions and parsley and cook for an additional 5 minutes, or until the mixture is no longer moist. Remove from the heat and let cool to the touch.

Spoon *half* the stuffing mixture into the hen cavity; reserve the remaining stuffing. Place the hen in an 8-inch-square baking dish that has been sprayed with nonstick vegetable cooking spray. Cover with aluminum foil and bake for 20 minutes. Uncover, and spoon the remaining stuffing mixture around the hen in the bottom of the dish. Return the hen to the oven and bake for 20 minutes longer, or until the hen is tender and golden brown.

PER SERVING	KCAL	FATgm	CHOLmg	SODmg
	224	7	79	370

CORNISH HEN À LA TRAYLOR

MAKES 2 SERVINGS

STEVE TRAYLOR is married to my daughter Toni, and he's one of our official taste testers. He loves everything Toni brings home, but has trouble believing so many of my Cajun dishes are low-calorie. He can hardly wait for the end of the day so he can sample my latest creation!

One 1-to-1½-pound
  Cornish game hen, skin
  and fat removed
2 *teaspoons ground*
  ginger
2 *teaspoons paprika*
¼ *teaspoon salt*
1 *teaspoon ground black*
  pepper

¼ *teaspoon ground white*
  pepper
¼ *teaspoon dried basil*
  leaves, crushed
¼ *teaspoon ground thyme*
2 *teaspoons browning*
  and seasoning sauce

Preheat the oven to 375°F.

Wash the hen and pat dry; set aside. In a small bowl, mix together all the dry ingredients. Sprinkle the seasoning over the hen and inside the cavity, using it all. Brush the entire hen with the browning sauce.

Spray the inside of an 8-inch-square baking dish with nonstick vegetable cooking spray. Place the hen in the dish and cover with aluminum foil. Bake for 20 minutes; baste the hen with the pan juices and bake, uncovered, for about 30 minutes longer, or until the hen is tender.

PER SERVING	KCAL	FATgm	CHOLmg	SODmg
	273	10	129	364

BEEF, PORK AND

OTHER MEATS

BEEF STEW

MAKES 4 SERVINGS

THIS OLD-TIME CAJUN FAVORITE is guaranteed to make your taste buds holler for more!

5 *cups water*
½ *cup Roux Flour*
   (page 18)
1 *cup chopped onions*
½ *teaspoon salt*
⅛ *teaspoon ground white*
   pepper
⅛ *teaspoon ground red*
   pepper

⅛ *teaspoon ground*
   oregano
1 *clove garlic, minced*
1 *bay leaf*
1 *pound round steak, cut*
   into 1-inch cubes

In a medium saucepan, combine the water and roux flour; place over high heat and bring to a boil, stirring often. Reduce the heat and add all the remaining ingredients. Cover and simmer for 1 hour, or until the meat is tender. Remove the bay leaf before serving.

PER SERVING	KCAL	FATgm	CHOLmg	SODmg
	274	7	92	330

MEATBALL STEW

MAKES 4 SERVINGS

THIS IS TRULY a Cajun dish. Cajun stews, which are different from stews in other parts of the country, are always made with roux to give them a rich gravy. Our stews are made with almost any meat or seafood—pork, chicken, crawfish, beef and shrimp are commonly used. My mom even used to make a potato stew without meat—and we loved it!

1 *pound ground beef*
1 *teaspoon salt*
1 *teaspoon ground white pepper*
½ *teaspoon granulated garlic*
¼ *teaspoon ground oregano*
4 *cups beef stock* or *water*

1 *cup Roux Flour (page 18)*
1 *cup chopped onions*
½ *cup chopped green bell pepper*
½ *cup chopped celery*
¼ *cup chopped green onions*
1 *tablespoon finely chopped fresh parsley*

In a large bowl, combine the beef, ½ teaspoon of the salt, ½ teaspoon of the white pepper, the garlic and oregano; mix well and shape into 8 meatballs.

In a 5-quart pot over high heat, bring the stock or water to a boil. Reduce the heat to medium; stir in the roux flour and the remaining salt and pepper and cook for 15 minutes, stirring often. Stir in the meatballs, onions, bell pepper and celery. Reduce heat to simmer; cover and cook 20 minutes longer. Remove from the heat and stir in the green onions and parsley. Cover and let stand for 5 minutes before serving.

PER SERVING	KCAL	FATgm	CHOLmg	SODmg
	324	8	92	586

CAJUN-STYLE CHILI

MAKES 4 SERVINGS

1 *pound ground beef*
½ *cup finely chopped*
  onions
¼ *teaspoon dried oregano*
  leaves, crushed
¼ *teaspoon curry powder*
¼ *teaspoon dry hot*
  mustard
¼ *teaspoon dried thyme*
  leaves, crushed
¼ *teaspoon minced fresh*
  garlic
1 *cup water*

2 *medium tomatoes,*
  peeled, seeded and
  chopped (about 1 cup)
2 *tablespoons quick-*
  mixing flour
One *6-ounce can tomato*
  juice
1 *teaspoon chili powder*
½ *teaspoon paprika*
⅛ *teaspoon ground black*
  pepper

Spray the inside of a large skillet with nonstick vegetable cooking spray and place over high heat. Add the beef and onions and sauté until brown, stirring constantly to prevent burning. Add the oregano, curry powder, mustard, thyme and garlic, then add ½ cup of the water and the tomatoes. Continue to cook, stirring, for about 5 minutes, or until thickened to the desired consistency. Stir in the flour and cook for 1 minute, stirring constantly. When the mixture starts to stick, add the remaining ½ cup water, the tomato juice, chili powder, paprika and pepper. Reduce the heat and simmer for 3 minutes before serving

PER SERVING	KCAL	FATgm	CHOLmg	SODmg
	258	7	92	98

SMOTHERED STEAK CARENCRO

MAKES 4 SERVINGS

*J*OUR RESTAURANT is located in Carencro, a small town north of Lafayette, Louisiana, that was named for the carrion crow, or buzzard. This recipe is named after the town, not the bird!

- 2 *tablespoons low-sodium soy sauce*
- 2 *tablespoons low-sodium Worcestershire sauce*
- ⅛ *teaspoon ground red pepper*
- ⅛ *teaspoon ground black pepper*
- ¾ *pound top round steak*
- 1 *medium onion, thinly sliced*
- 1 *medium green bell pepper, thinly sliced*
- 2 *teaspoons quick-mixing flour*
- 1½ *cups water*
- 2 *medium tomatoes, peeled, seeded and chopped (about 1 cup)*
- ⅓ *cup finely chopped green onions*
- 2 *cups hot cooked rice*

In a medium bowl, combine the soy sauce, Worcestershire and red and black peppers. Pour over the steak and marinate in the refrigerator for 1 hour.

Spray the inside of a heavy skillet with nonstick vegetable cooking spray; place over high heat until the skillet is very hot, but not smoking. Add the steak and cook until brown on both sides, about 10 or 15 minutes, turning often to prevent burning. Add the onion and bell pepper, reduce the heat to medium and continue cooking for 10 minutes, stirring often.

When the mixture starts to stick to the bottom of the skillet, stir in the flour. Gradually pour in ¼ cup of the water, stirring constantly. Cook until all the liquid has evaporated, about 10 minutes; add the remaining 1¼ cups water, the tomatoes and green onions. Cook for 10 minutes and serve over the rice.

PER SERVING	KCAL	FATgm	CHOLmg	SODmg
	314	6	69	126

SWEET-AND-SOUR STEAK

MAKES 2 SERVINGS

½ *pound top round steak, cut into ½-inch strips*
1 *small onion, thinly sliced*
1 *small green bell pepper, thinly sliced*
1 *cup water*
2 *teaspoons cornstarch*
¼ *cup unsweetened pineapple juice*
¼ *teaspoon brown sugar substitute*
⅛ *teaspoon salt*
⅛ *teaspoon ground red pepper*

⅛ *teaspoon ground black pepper*
⅛ *teaspoon peeled and grated ginger*
¼ *cup canned pineapple chunks, packed in their own juices*
2 *tablespoons white vinegar*
2 *tablespoons lemon juice*
1 *tablespoon low-sodium soy sauce*
1 *tablespoon low-sodium Worcestershire sauce*

Spray the inside of a medium, heavy skillet with nonstick vegetable cooking spray. Place over high heat and heat until very hot, but not smoking. Add the meat and sauté for 3 minutes, or until brown, stirring constantly to prevent burning. Add the onion and bell pepper and sauté, stirring, for about 10 minutes. When the mixture starts to stick to the skillet, stir in the water; continue cooking for about 10 minutes longer.

Meanwhile in a small bowl, dissolve the cornstarch in the pineapple juice. When all the liquid in the skillet has evaporated, stir in the dissolved cornstarch. Stir in all the remaining ingredients and reduce the heat; simmer, uncovered, for 20 minutes, or until the meat is tender and the gravy thickened.

PER SERVING	KCAL	FATgm	CHOLmg	SODmg
	309	7	92	536

MACARONI WITH MEAT SAUCE

MAKES EIGHT ½-CUP SERVINGS

1½ cups uncooked
   macaroni
2 cups finely chopped
   onions
½ cup finely chopped
   green bell pepper
½ cup finely chopped
   celery
1 pound ground beef
1 teaspoon salt
2 teaspoons chili powder
½ teaspoon ground
   oregano
½ teaspoon granulated
   garlic

½ teaspoon dried basil
   leaves, crushed
¼ teaspoon ground white
   pepper
¼ teaspoon ground red
   pepper
2 cups beef stock or
   water
½ cup tomato paste
4 medium tomatoes
   peeled, seeded and
   cubed (about 2 cups)
¼ cup finely chopped
   fresh parsley

Cook the macaroni according to package directions, omitting
the salt; drain and set aside.

Spray the inside of a 4-quart pot with nonstick vegetable cooking spray and place over high heat. Add the onions, bell pepper
and celery; sauté for 5 minutes, stirring constantly to prevent
burning. Add the beef and the next 7 ingredients. Cook, stirring,
for 15 minutes, then stir in the stock, tomato paste and tomatoes.
Cover, reduce the heat and simmer for 15 minutes, stirring often.
Add the macaroni and cook for 8 minutes; remove from the heat.
Stir in the parsley and let stand for 10 minutes, allowing the
macaroni to absorb the meat flavor.

PER SERVING	KCAL	FATgm	CHOLmg	SODmg
	359	4	46	313

STUFFED BELL PEPPERS A LA KATHY

MAKES 6 SERVINGS

THIS RECIPE is named for my daughter-in-law Kathy.

3 *medium whole green bell peppers*
1 *quart water*
1 *pound ground chuck*
1 *cup very finely chopped onions*
½ *cup very finely chopped green bell pepper*
½ *cup very finely chopped celery*
2 *medium tomatoes, peeled, seeded and chopped (about 1 cup)*
¼ *teaspoon salt*
½ *teaspoon granulated garlic*
½ *teaspoon chili powder*
½ *teaspoon paprika*

½ *teaspoon ground red pepper*
¼ *cup very finely chopped green onions*
¼ *cup shredded reduced-fat Cheddar cheese*
2 *slices bread (40 calories per slice), cut into ½-inch cubes*
2 *egg whites*
¼ *cup evaporated skim milk*
½ *cup Chicken Stock (page 20) or water*
2 *tablespoons fine dry bread crumbs*

Preheat the oven to 350°F.

Cut the whole bell peppers in half lengthwise. Remove the top stems and seeds and discard. In a medium saucepan over high heat, bring the water to a boil. Add the bell peppers and boil for 5 to 7 minutes or until crisp-tender; drain and set aside.

Spray the inside of a medium skillet with nonstick vegetable cooking spray and place over high heat. Add the ground chuck, onions, chopped bell pepper and celery and sauté, stirring, for

10 minutes. Add the tomatoes and dry seasonings; cook, stirring, for 5 minutes longer.

Remove from the heat and add green onions, cheese and bread cubes, stirring well. In a small bowl, beat together the egg whites and milk. Slowly add to the meat mixture, stirring constantly.

Spray the inside of an 8-inch-square baking dish with nonstick vegetable cooking spray. Spoon *half* the meat mixture into the dish, spreading evenly. Fill each bell pepper half with the remaining meat mixture, then arrange the peppers in the dish and pour in stock.

Sprinkle some of the bread crumbs over each bell pepper. Cover with aluminum foil and bake for 15 minutes. Uncover and bake for 20 minutes longer.

PER SERVING	KCAL	FATgm	CHOLmg	SODmg
	222	6	64	249

PEPPER-RICE BEEF

MAKES 4 SERVINGS

WHEN I WAS A CHILD, we had this dish often. It was so quick and easy that we children sometimes fixed it ourselves for a snack. I've been making it since I was nine years old.

1 *pound ground beef*
⅛ *teaspoon salt*
⅛ *teaspoon ground white pepper*
⅓ *cup chopped green bell pepper*

⅓ *cup chopped red bell pepper*
⅓ *cup finely chopped green onions*
½ *cup beef stock or water*
2 *cups hot cooked rice*

Spray the inside of a large skillet with nonstick vegetable cooking spray. Add the beef and place over medium heat; cook for 3 minutes, stirring often. Add the salt, white pepper and bell peppers; continue cooking for 8 minutes, stirring constantly to prevent burning. Add the green onions, stock and rice. Cook, stirring, for 2 minutes more. Remove from the heat and let stand for 2 minutes before serving. (This allows the rice to absorb some of the flavor.)

PER SERVING	KCAL	FATgm	CHOLmg	SODmg
	315	7	92	140

MARINATED GRILLADES

MAKES 4 SERVINGS

GRILLADES are small pieces of beef or pork, "smothered" in a brown gravy. It's real Cajun and real good!

½ cup chopped onions
1 tablespoon cider
   vinegar
1 tablespoon olive oil
1 tablespoon low-sodium
   Worcestershire sauce
1 teaspoon ground red
   pepper
1 teaspoon dried
   tarragon leaves,
   crushed

½ teaspoon salt
½ teaspoon granulated
   garlic
⅛ teaspoon dried basil
   leaves, crushed
⅛ teaspoon ground thyme
⅛ teaspoon ground
   oregano
1½ pounds flank steak, cut
   into 1-inch cubes
1½ cups water

In a small bowl, combine all the ingredients except for the meat and water; mix well. Place the meat in a large bowl and pour in the marinade, mixing well. Cover and refrigerate for 7 hours or overnight.

In a large skillet over medium heat, cook the meat with the marinade, covered, for 15 minutes, stirring often, until the meat is brown on all sides. Add the water and reduce the heat; simmer, covered, for 30 minutes, or until the meat is tender.

PER SERVING	KCAL	FATgm	CHOLmg	SODmg
	370	14	138	375

PORK TENDERLOIN

MAKES 2 SERVINGS

AFTER TASTING THIS DISH, a friend replied, "When will the cookbook be complete?"

⅛ *teaspoon salt*
¼ *teaspoon ground white pepper*
¼ *teaspoon celery seeds*
¼ *teaspoon ground red pepper*
¼ *teaspoon chili powder*
¼ *teaspoon paprika*
4 *pork tenderloins (1 ounce each)*
1 *cup very finely chopped onions*

1 *teaspoon cornstarch*
1 *tablespoon dry sherry*
One-half 5-ounce can *condensed salt-free beef consommé*
4 *thinly sliced green bell pepper rings*
4 *thinly sliced red bell pepper rings*

In a small bowl, combine the first 6 ingredients. Mix well and sprinkle over both sides of the pork; set aside.

Spray the inside of a medium skillet with nonstick vegetable cooking spray and heat till very hot over high heat. Add the pork and cook for 10 minutes, or until brown on both sides, turning often. Transfer to a plate and keep warm.

Spray same skillet again with nonstick vegetable cooking spray and place over medium heat. Add the onions and cook for 2 minutes, stirring often. Dissolve the cornstarch in the sherry and add to the skillet along with the consommé and bell pepper rings. Cook for 5 minutes, or until the sauce thickens. Spoon the sauce over the pork and top each one with bell peppers.

PER SERVING	KCAL	FATgm	CHOLmg	SODmg
	156	3	53	247

MARINATED PORK KABOBS

MAKES 4 SERVINGS

½ *pound boneless pork tenderloin, cut into 1-inch cubes*
16 *small fresh mushrooms*
1 *medium green bell pepper, cut into 2-inch squares*
1 *medium onion, quartered*
16 *cherry tomatoes*

¼ *cup red wine*
2 *teaspoons low-sodium teriyaki sauce*
¼ *teaspoon salt*
¼ *teaspoon granulated garlic*
¼ *teaspoon ground oregano*
¼ *teaspoon curry powder*

Place the pork, mushrooms, bell pepper, onion and tomatoes in a plastic bag. Combine the wine, teriyaki sauce, salt, garlic, oregano and curry powder and mix well. Pour into the plastic bag; seal and shake well. Refrigerate for at least 3 hours.

Meanwhile soak 4 wooden skewers in cold water (this will prevent their burning). Arrange the marinated meat and vegetables on the skewers, then spray with nonstick vegetable cooking spray. Place the skewered meat and vegetables on a hot grill, turning often and brushing with the remaining marinade. Grill for 15 minutes, or until the meat is tender.

PER SERVING	KCAL	FATgm	CHOLmg	SODmg
	127	3	53	276

PORK STEAK WITH WINE SAUCE

MAKES 4 SERVINGS

Four 5-ounce boneless
  pork tenderloins
⅛ *teaspoon salt*
⅛ *teaspoon ground black*
  pepper
1 *cup thinly sliced fresh*
  mushrooms
½ *cup chopped red bell*
  pepper

¼ *cup chopped green*
  onions
½ *teaspoon cornstarch*
½ *cup dry red wine*
½ *teaspoon finely*
  chopped fresh parsley

Spray the inside of a medium skillet with nonstick vegetable cooking spray and place over high heat. Season the pork with the salt and pepper. Add the pork and sauté until the meat is brown. Remove from the heat, transfer to a warm platter and keep warm.

Spray the same skillet again with nonstick vegetable cooking spray. Add the mushrooms, bell pepper and green onions; cook over medium heat, stirring, for 5 minutes. Dissolve the cornstarch in the wine. Add the dissolved cornstarch and wine and parsley; cook for an additional 3 minutes. Serve over the steaks.

PER SERVING	KCAL	FATgm	CHOLmg	SODmg
	264	7	131	176

STIR-FRIED PORK

MAKES 4 SERVINGS

1 *pound boneless pork tenderloin, cut into ¼-inch strips*
¼ *teaspoon salt*
½ *teaspoon ground white pepper*
½ *teaspoon granulated garlic*
½ *teaspoon ground red pepper*
½ *teaspoon chili powder*
3 *tablespoons low-sodium soy sauce*
1 *tablespoon low-sodium Worcestershire sauce*

3 *teaspoons cornstarch*
2 *cups beef stock or water*
1 *small zucchini, cut into julienne*
1 *small yellow squash, cut into julienne*
½ *medium onion, thinly sliced*
1 *cup fresh broccoli florets*
1 *cup fresh cauliflowerets*
4 *thinly sliced red bell pepper rings*

Spray the inside of a large skillet with nonstick vegetable cooking spray and place over high heat. Add the meat and sauté, stirring, for 10 minutes. Add the next 7 ingredients; cook for 10 minutes longer, stirring often. Dissolve the cornstarch in stock and add to the skillet along with all the remaining ingredients, stirring well. Cook for 10 minutes, or until sauce thickens, stirring occasionally.

PER SERVING	KCAL	FATgm	CHOLmg	SODmg
	237	6	105	435

BLACKENED PORK CHOP

MAKES 1 SERVING

⅛ *teaspoon paprika*
½ *teaspoon salt*
¼ *teaspoon ground red*
   pepper
¼ *teaspoon ground cumin*
¼ *teaspoon ground*
   oregano

⅛ *teaspoon ground white*
   pepper
⅛ *teaspoon onion powder*
One 6-ounce pork chop

Preheat the oven to 350°F.

Heat a medium cast-iron skillet over high heat for 15 minutes, or until very hot. Meanwhile, in a small bowl, combine the seasonings; mix well and set aside.

Spray both sides of the pork chop with nonstick vegetable cooking spray and sprinkle one side with *half* the seasoning. Place seasoned side down in the skillet and cook for 1½ minutes. Meanwhile quickly sprinkle the remaining seasoning over the top side of pork chop. When 1½ minutes is up, turn the pork chop and cook for 1½ minutes more. Remove from the skillet and place on a small baking sheet that has been sprayed with nonstick vegetable cooking spray. Bake for 20 minutes.

PER SERVING	KCAL	FATgm	CHOLmg	SODmg
	291	9	158	360

CRABMEAT-STUFFED PORK LOIN

MAKES 4 SERVINGS

⅛ teaspoon salt
⅛ teaspoon ground white pepper
⅛ teaspoon ground red pepper
⅛ teaspoon ground thyme
1 pound boneless pork loin
½ cup finely chopped onions
½ cup finely chopped green bell pepper

½ cup beef stock or water
1 teaspoon low-sodium soy sauce
1 teaspoon lemon juice
2 slices stale bread (40 calories per slice), cut into ½-inch cubes
½ pound fresh lump crabmeat, picked over

Preheat the oven to 350°F.

In a small bowl, combine the salt, white pepper, red pepper and thyme; mix well and set aside.

Place the pork on a flat surface and cut a deep 3-inch-long slit in the center to form a pocket, being careful not to cut all the way through the meat. Sprinkle the seasoning mix on the outside surface and inside the pocket; set aside.

Spray the inside of a medium skillet with nonstick vegetable cooking spray and place over high heat. Add the onions and bell pepper and sauté for 5 minutes, stirring often. Add the stock and the remaining seasoning mix. Reduce the heat to simmer; stir in the soy sauce, lemon juice, bread cubes and crabmeat. Cook for 1 minute, or until the mixture is firm but not dry. Remove from the heat. Spoon into the pocket and secure with toothpicks.

Spray the inside of an 8-inch-square baking dish with nonstick vegetable cooking spray. Place the pork in the dish and cover with aluminum foil. Bake for 30 minutes, turning once during cooking. Uncover and cook for 10 minutes more. Turn the pork over and cook for 10 minutes longer, or until brown. Remove the toothpicks before serving.

PER SERVING	KCAL	FATgm	CHOLmg	SODmg
	268	6	138	472

VEAL MEDALLIONS IN DILL-WINE SAUCE

MAKES 2 SERVINGS

THE BLEND of seasonings and wine makes this dish unique!

½ *pound boneless veal shoulder steak*
¼ *teaspoon salt*
½ *teaspoon sweet paprika*
¼ *teaspoon dried dillweed*
⅛ *teaspoon ground white pepper*
⅛ *teaspoon ground black pepper*

1 *tablespoon dehydrated onion*
¼ *cup finely chopped green onions*
1½ *cups Chicken Stock (page 20) or water*
⅓ *cup evaporated skim milk*
¼ *cup dry white wine*
2 *tablespoons cornstarch*

Trim all visible fat from the veal and pound to a ⅛-inch thickness; cut into medallions 2 inches in diameter.

In a small bowl, combine the next 6 dry ingredients; mix well and sprinkle on both sides of the meat. Spray the inside of a medium skillet with nonstick vegetable cooking spray and place over high heat. Add meat and sauté for 5 minutes on each side. Remove from the heat and transfer to a plate; keep warm.

Return the same skillet to medium heat and add the dehydrated onion and green onions; cook for 1 minute, stirring constantly to prevent burning. Add *1 cup* of the stock, the milk and wine.

Dissolve the cornstarch in remaining ½ cup stock and gradually stir into the skillet. Cook for 10 minutes, or until the sauce thickens. Remove from the heat and spoon half the sauce onto each of 2 plates. Place half the meat on each plate and serve immediately.

PER SERVING	KCAL	FATgm	CHOLmg	SODmg
	204	5	2	661

OVEN-FRIED VEAL WITH "CREAM" SAUCE

MAKES 4 SERVINGS

CRISPY BATTERED VEAL topped with a smooth, creamy sauce.

⅛ *teaspoon salt*
⅛ *teaspoon ground white pepper*
⅛ *teaspoon ground oregano*
⅛ *teaspoon ground sage*
Four ⅛-*inch-thick veal cutlets (about 2 ounces each)*
1 *cup evaporated skim milk*

6 *tablespoons plain low-fat yogurt*
¼ *cup fine dry bread crumbs*
¼ *cup dehydrated onion*
1 *tablespoon finely chopped fresh parsley*
2 *teaspoons quick-mixing flour*
1 *teaspoon butter-flavored sprinkles*

Preheat the oven to 350°F.

In a small bowl, combine the salt, pepper, oregano and sage; mix well and sprinkle over both sides of the veal; set aside. In a medium bowl, combine ¼ cup of the milk and 3 tablespoons of the yogurt and beat until smooth; set aside.

Spray the inside of a large skillet with nonstick vegetable cooking spray. Place over high heat for 2 minutes, or until the skillet is very hot, then reduce the heat to medium. Dip each veal fillet in the yogurt-milk mixture, then dredge in the bread crumbs. Sauté for 1 minute, turning often to prevent burning. Transfer to a baking dish; bake for 5 minutes while preparing the sauce.

Spray the inside of a small skillet with nonstick vegetable cooking spray and place over high heat. Add the remaining 3 tablespoons yogurt and ¾ cup milk and bring to a boil. Reduce the heat and simmer, stirring, for 1 minute, or until the sauce begins to thicken. Stir in the onion, parsley and flour and cook for 2 minutes. Add the butter-flavored sprinkles; stir well and remove from the heat. Place the veal on individual plates and top with the sauce.

PER SERVING	KCAL	FATgm	CHOLmg	SODmg
	157	4	4	243

LAMB STEW

MAKES 4 SERVINGS

SERVE THIS STEW over hot cooked rice. It tastes better when prepared 1 day ahead and then reheated.

1 *quart water*
1 *pound boneless lamb shoulder, cut into 1-inch cubes*
½ *cup Roux Flour (page 18)*
1 *cup finely chopped onions*
½ *cup finely chopped green bell pepper*

½ *cup finely chopped celery*
½ *teaspoon salt*
½ *teaspoon ground thyme*
¼ *teaspoon ground red pepper*
2 *cups hot cooked rice*

In a large saucepan over high heat, bring the water to a boil. Add the lamb, roux flour, onions, bell pepper and celery. Reduce the heat to medium; cover, and simmer for 15 minutes, stirring occasionally. Add the salt, thyme and red pepper. Simmer, covered, for 15 minutes. Serve hot over rice.

PER SERVING	KCAL	FATgm	CHOLmg	SODmg
	293	11	119	344

BLACKENED LAMB CHOP

MAKES 2 SERVINGS

½ *teaspoon paprika*
⅛ *teaspoon salt*
¼ *teaspoon ground cumin*
¼ *teaspoon ground oregano*
¼ *teaspoon ground red pepper*

⅛ *teaspoon ground white pepper*
⅛ *teaspoon onion powder*
2 *lamb chops (about 4 ounces each)*

Preheat the oven to 350°F.

Heat a medium cast-iron skillet over high heat for 15 minutes, or until very hot. Meanwhile, in a small bowl, combine the seasonings; mix well and set aside.

Spray both sides of the lamb chops with nonstick vegetable cooking spray and sprinkle one side with *half* the seasoning. Place seasoned side down in the skillet and cook for 1½ minutes.

Meanwhile quickly sprinkle the remaining seasoning over the top side of the lamb chop. When 1½ minutes is up, turn the lamb chops and cook for 1½ minutes more. Remove from the skillet and place on a small baking sheet that has been sprayed with nonstick vegetable cooking spray. Bake for 15 minutes.

PER SERVING	KCAL	FATgm	CHOLmg	SODmg
	244	12	111	323

RABBIT SAUCE PIQUANT

MAKES 6 SERVINGS

RABBIT is low in fat and can be served many ways, but cooked in this sauce piquant, it's dynamite!

½ *teaspoon salt*
1 *teaspoon ground white pepper*
1 *teaspoon ground red pepper*
One *2½-pound rabbit, cut into 6 pieces*
2 *cups finely chopped onions*
½ *cup finely chopped green bell pepper*

⅓ *cup finely chopped celery*
3 *tablespoons tomato paste*
3 *cups Chicken Stock (page 20) or water*
2 *tablespoons Roux Flour (page 18)*
⅓ *cup finely chopped green onions*

Sprinkle the salt and white and red peppers on both sides of the rabbit. Spray a medium pot with nonstick vegetable cooking spray and place over high heat. Add the rabbit and cook for 30 minutes, until thoroughly brown on all sides, turning often. Add the onions, bell pepper, celery and tomato paste; continue cooking for 10 minutes, stirring often to prevent burning.

Reduce the heat to medium and add the stock and roux flour; cover and cook for 25 minutes. Reduce the heat, stir in the green onions and simmer, covered, for 5 minutes.

PER SERVING	KCAL	FATgm	CHOLmg	SODmg
	135	2	No data	205

VEGETABLES

OVERNIGHT BUTTER BEANS

MAKES 6 SERVINGS

WHAT WE CALL BUTTER BEANS in the South, you may know as dried lima beans. Soaking the beans overnight cuts the cooking time in half.

1 *cup dried butter beans*
6 *cups hot water*
½ *cup finely chopped*
   onions
½ *teaspoon salt*

½ *teaspoon ground white*
   pepper
⅓ *cup chopped green*
   onions

Pick through the beans and discard any small pebbles; rinse well. Place in a large saucepan, cover with cold water to 2 inches above the beans. Let stand overnight; drain.

In the large saucepan combine the beans, the 6 cups hot water and onions, cover and cook over medium heat for 1 hour. Add the salt, pepper and green onions. Reduce heat and simmer for 15 minutes, or until the beans are tender, stirring occasionally.

PER SERVING	KCAL	FATgm	CHOLmg	SODmg
	40	0.1	0	178

COUNTRY LIMAS WITH HAM

MAKES 4 SERVINGS

MOM AND DAD always planted lima beans in our garden, so we learned to fix them many different ways, such as in this recipe with ham. Some people like their beans with a hint of sweetness. Add a little sugar substitute after the beans are cooked and let them stand a few minutes before serving.

One 1-pound package frozen lima beans, thawed or 1 pound fresh shelled lima beans
2 cups water
1 cup reduced-fat chopped ham, cubed

1 cup finely chopped onions
¼ cup finely chopped green bell pepper
¼ cup finely chopped celery
¼ teaspoon ground white pepper

In a large saucepan, combine all the ingredients. Bring to a boil. Reduce the heat to medium, cover, and cook for 30 minutes, or until the beans are tender, stirring occasionally and mashing some of the beans against the side of the saucepan to make a "thick sauce."

PER SERVING	KCAL	FATgm	CHOLmg	SODmg
	178	2	10	474

SUMMER GREEN BEAN CASSEROLE

MAKES 4 SERVINGS

THIS CASSEROLE is so rich and creamy, you'll want to fix it often. It's also a great way to get youngsters to eat their beans.

3 *cups fresh green beans, cut into 1½-inch pieces*
½ *cup evaporated skim milk*
2 *tablespoons chopped green bell pepper*
1 *tablespoon chopped red bell pepper*
1 *tablespoon minced fresh onion*

½ *teaspoon salt*
¼ *teaspoon ground white pepper*
¼ *teaspoon ground thyme*
¼ *teaspoon dried basil leaves, crushed*

Preheat the oven to 350°F.

In a medium saucepan, bring 2 cups water to a boil. Add the beans and return to a boil; cover, reduce heat and cook for 5 minutes, or until the beans are crisp-tender. Drain the beans well and transfer to a 1-quart casserole dish.

In a small bowl, mix together the remaining ingredients and pour over the beans. Cover and bake for 1 hour, stirring once after 30 minutes. Serve hot.

PER SERVING	KCAL	FATgm	CHOLmg	SODmg
	62	0.40	1	288

SNAP BEANS WITH POTATOES

J IN THE SOUTH we call them snap beans instead of green beans. But whatever they're called they're great—especially when combined with potatoes.

2 *cups fresh snap beans*
1 *medium potato, peeled and cut into 1-inch cubes (about ½ cup)*
½ *cup finely chopped onions*
½ *cup finely chopped green bell pepper*

¼ *teaspoon salt*
¼ *teaspoon granulated garlic*
⅛ *teaspoon ground white pepper*
1 *teaspoon butter-flavored granules*

In a medium saucepan over high heat, bring 1 quart water to a boil. Stir in all the ingredients except for the butter-flavored granules. Reduce the heat to medium, cover and cook for 15 minutes. Uncover, increase the heat to high and cook for 15 minutes, stirring often. Drain the vegetables well, pour into a serving dish and top with the butter-flavored granules.

PER SERVING	KCAL	FATgm	CHOLmg	SODmg
	102	0.48	0	201

WHOLE SNAP BEANS

MAKES 3 SERVINGS

A TASTY SIDE DISH. Serve with meat, poultry or fish.

½ *pound fresh snap beans*
¼ *cup finely chopped*
   onions
¼ *cup finely chopped green*
   bell pepper
⅛ *teaspoon salt*
⅛ *teaspoon ground black*
   pepper
1 *cup liquid reserved from*
   the beans

1 *tablespoon salt-free*
   chicken bouillon
   granules
½ *teaspoon butter-*
   flavored granules
1 *tablespoon finely*
   chopped green
   onions
1 *teaspoon dried basil*
   leaves, crushed

In a medium saucepan over high heat, bring 2 cups water to a boil. Add the beans and return to a boil. Reduce the heat to medium; cover, and cook for 20 minutes, or until crisp-tender. Drain, reserving 1 cup liquid and set aside.

Spray the inside of a medium heavy skillet with nonstick vegetable cooking spray and place over medium heat. Add the beans, onions, bell pepper, salt and black pepper. Cook for 3 minutes, stirring often. Stir in the reserved liquid, bouillon and butter-flavored granules; cook for 1 minute longer, then stir in the green onions and basil. Remove from the heat and let stand 5 minutes before serving.

PER SERVING	KCAL	FATgm	CHOLmg	SODmg
	57	1	2	108

FIELD PEAS WITH SNAPS

MAKES 6 SERVINGS

DELICIOUS AS IS or when combined with a cup of hot cooked rice. If field peas are unavailable in your area, substitute peas.

One 1-pound package frozen field peas with snaps
2½ cups water
1 cup finely chopped onions
½ teaspoon salt
1 teaspoon minced fresh garlic
¼ teaspoon ground white pepper
¼ teaspoon ground oregano
¼ cup finely chopped green onions
⅛ teaspoon very finely chopped fresh parsley

In a large saucepan over high heat, combine all the ingredients except for the green onions and parsley and bring to a boil. Reduce the heat, cover and simmer for 30 minutes, stirring occasionally. Stir in the green onions and parsley and cook for 15 minutes.

PER SERVING	KCAL	FATgm	CHOLmg	SODmg
	111	0.6	0	171

FIELD PEAS WITH JALAPENO AND TURKEY

MAKES 6 SERVINGS

SERVE THIS as a side dish or with rice for a hearty main meal.

One 1-pound package
  frozen field peas
2½ cups Chicken Stock
  (page 20) or water
1 cup finely chopped
  onions
½ cup finely chopped
  celery
¼ teaspoon salt

¼ teaspoon ground white
  pepper
1 bay leaf
¼ cup sliced mild
  jalapeño peppers
1 pound cooked turkey
  breast, cut into
  ½-inch cubes

In a large saucepan over high heat, combine all the ingredients except for the jalepeño and turkey. Cover, and cook for 20 minutes, stirring occasionally. Reduce the heat to medium and add the jalapeño and turkey; cook, uncovered for 20 minutes longer, or until the turkey is tender. Remove the bay leaf before serving.

PER SERVING	KCAL	FATgm	CHOLmg	SODmg
	195	1	63	173

WHITE BEANS WITH CANADIAN BACON

MAKES 4 SERVINGS

A GREAT SIDE DISH. Adding bacon to the beans creates a unique flavor.

1½ cups dried white beans
3 cups hot water
2 ounces Canadian bacon, chopped
1 cup finely chopped onions

½ cup finely chopped celery
1 teaspoon minced fresh garlic
½ teaspoon ground white pepper

Sort the beans and rinse well; place in a large saucepan and cover with cold water. Let soak overnight, then drain.

The next day, combine the beans, hot water, and all the remaining ingredients in the same saucepan and place over medium heat. Cover, and cook for 1½ hours, or until the beans are tender, stirring often.

PER SERVING	KCAL	FATgm	CHOLmg	SODmg
	124	2	8.21	243

BLACK-EYED PEAS DIANE

MAKES 6 SERVINGS

THIS RECIPE is named for my oldest daughter, Diane. As a child she was often ill, but I always knew when she was on the road to recovery because she would get hungry for black-eyed peas!

½	**pound dried black-eyed peas**	1	**bay leaf**
1½	**quarts water**	½	**teaspoon salt**
1	**cup finely chopped onions**	½	**teaspoon ground red pepper**

Place the peas in a large saucepan and add enough water to cover. Soak for 8 hours or overnight, then drain.

Add the 1½ quarts water to the peas and place over high heat; bring to a boil. Reduce the heat to medium and add the onions, bay leaf, salt and red pepper. Cook for 1 hour, uncovered, or until the peas are tender, stirring often. Mash some of the peas with the back of a spoon to make a thicker gravy.

PER SERVING	KCAL	FATgm	CHOLmg	SODmg
	51	0.40	0	172

CROWDER PEA LEIGH

MAKES 8 SERVINGS

MY GRANDDAUGHTER LEIGH loved this dish, so I named it after her. Crowder peas are dried, tan-colored peas. Substitute black-eyed peas if you can't find crowder peas.

One 16-ounce package
    frozen crowder peas
3 cups water
1 cup finely chopped
    onions
1 cup finely chopped
    green bell pepper
½ cup finely chopped
    celery

1 teaspoon salt
½ teaspoon ground
    marjoram
⅛ teaspoon ground red
    pepper
1 clove garlic, minced

In a large saucepan over high heat, bring the peas and water to a boil. Reduce the heat to medium and add the onions, bell pepper and celery; cover, and cook for 30 minutes, stirring often. Reduce the heat to simmer and stir in all the remaining ingredients. Continue cooking, covered, for 30 minutes longer.

PER SERVING	KCAL	FATgm	CHOLmg	SODmg
	71	0.5	0	258

PEAS-THAT-MAKE-YOU-CRAZY

MAKES 6 SERVINGS

BROTHER PAUL serves a similar dish in his restaurant; I took out some of the high-calorie ingredients. Whatever version you eat, these peas will really make your taste buds go crazy!

¼ *pound boneless pork tenderloin, cubed (about ½ cup)*
¼ *pound boneless turkey breast, cubed (about ½ cup)*
3 *cups water*
¾ *cup dried black-eyed peas*
1 *cup chopped onions*
1 *small whole jalapeño pepper, seeds removed*

½ *teaspoon salt*
¼ *teaspoon ground white pepper*
⅛ *teaspoon ground black pepper*
⅛ *teaspoon celery seed*
1 *bay leaf*
3 *cups hot cooked rice*

Spray the inside of a medium skillet with nonstick vegetable cooking spray and place over high heat. Add the pork and turkey and sauté for 5 minutes, or until the meat is well-browned, stirring often to prevent sticking, transfer the meat to a slow cooker. Stir in all the remaining ingredients. Cover, and cook on high heat for 3½ hours, or until the peas and meat are tender. Remove the jalapeño and bay leaf before serving. Serve over hot cooked rice.

PER SERVING	KCAL	FATgm	CHOLmg	SODmg
	153	1	33	200

RED BEANS WITH TURKEY SAUSAGE

MAKES 6 SERVINGS

YOU CAN'T GET more Cajun than red beans.

1 *pound dried red beans*
1 *pound Smoked Turkey*
   Sausage (page 110), cut
   into 2-inch pieces
2 *quarts hot water*
1 *cup finely chopped*
   onions

½ *cup finely chopped*
   green bell pepper
½ *cup finely chopped*
   celery
1 *teaspoon ground red*
   pepper
½ *teaspoon salt*
1 *bay leaf*

In a large pot, place the beans and enough water to cover by 2 inches; Soak the beans overnight. Drain thoroughly.

To the same pot over medium heat add all the remaining ingredients. Cover, and cook for 30 minutes, stirring often. Reduce the heat and simmer for 30 minutes longer, or until the beans are tender. Remove the bay leaf and serve.

PER SERVING	KCAL	FATgm	CHOLmg	SODmg
	218	1.28	63	228

WHITE BEANS

MAKES 6 SERVINGS

THIS IS A GREAT SIDE DISH with meat, poultry or fish. For a hearty main course, allow 2 cups beans with 1 cup cooked rice.

1 *pound dried white beans*
7 *cups hot water*
1 *cup finely chopped onions*
½ *cup finely chopped green bell pepper*
½ *cup finely chopped celery*

1 *teaspoon salt*
1 *teaspoon ground white pepper*
¼ *teaspoon ground marjoram*
⅛ *teaspoon ground cumin*
3 *cups hot cooked rice (optional)*

Place the beans in a large pot and add enough water to cover; let soak for 8 hours or overnight. Drain thoroughly.

In the same pot over medium heat, combine the beans and the hot water. Cover, and cook for 30 minutes, stirring often. Add all the remaining ingredients; continue cooking, covered, for 30 minutes longer, or until the beans are tender, stirring occasionally. Mash some of the beans against the inside of pot with a spoon; this makes a rich, thick gravy.

PER CUP	KCAL	FATgm	CHOLmg	SODmg
	101	0.5	0	186

C'EST BON! BEETS

MAKES 3 SERVINGS

**One 16-ounce can sliced
beets
One-half 6-ounce can
frozen orange juice
concentrate, undiluted**

**2 packets sugar substitute
2 teaspoons grated orange
peel**

Drain the beets, reserving ½ cup of the liquid; place the beets in a small bowl and set aside. In a small skillet over low heat, combine the reserved beet juice and orange juice concentrate. Cook for 3 minutes, stirring often. Remove from the heat and stir in the sugar substitute and orange peel. Let stand for 5 minutes, then pour over the beets.

PER SERVING	KCAL	FATgm	CHOLmg	SODmg
	72	0.22	0	73

OLD-FASHIONED PICKLED BEETS

MAKES 4 SERVINGS

THIS RECIPE is an old favorite of mine. Serve the beets with meat, poultry or fish.

One 16-ounce can sliced beets
½ small onion, sliced and separated into rings
2 tablespoons tarragon vinegar or cider vinegar

⅛ teaspoon ground white pepper
3 packets sugar substitute

Drain the beets, reserving ½ of the liquid. Spray the inside of a medium skillet with nonstick vegetable cooking spray and place over medium heat; add the beets, reserved liquid, onion rings, vinegar and white pepper. Cook for 3 minutes, stirring often. Remove from heat and stir in the sugar substitute. Serve hot.

PER SERVING	KCAL	FATgm	CHOLmg	SODmg
	36	0.08	0	54

SMOTHERED OKRA WITH TOMATOES

MAKES 2 SERVINGS

IF FRESH OKRA is unavailable, substitute frozen.

1 *tablespoon reduced-calorie margarine*
1 *tablespoon olive oil*
1 *pound fresh okra, cut into ¼-inch slices*
¼ *teaspoon salt*
¼ *teaspoon ground cumin*
¼ *teaspoon ground white pepper*

¼ *teaspoon ground red pepper*
1 *medium tomato, peeled, seeded and chopped (about ½ cup)*
1 *teaspoon paprika*
½ *cup water*

In a large skillet over high heat, heat the margarine and olive oil until very hot. Add the okra, salt, cumin and white and red pepper; stir constantly to prevent sticking. Cook for about 15 minutes, or until the okra is no longer slimy, then add the tomato and paprika. Reduce the heat to medium and continue cooking. When the okra starts to stick, scrape the bottom of the skillet with a spoon; continue cooking and stirring until the okra turns a light brown color. Gradually stir in the water. Cook, uncovered, for about 30 minutes longer, or until all the liquid has evaporated, stirring often.

PER SERVING	KCAL	FATgm	CHOLmg	SODmg
	143	7	0	333

SMOTHERED OKRA WITH MUSHROOMS

MAKES 2 SERVINGS

IN THE SOUTH we can hardly wait until the fresh okra is ready to be picked, but until then, we've come up with some tasty ways to use frozen okra!

1 *tablespoon vegetable oil*
One *1-pound package frozen cut okra, thawed*
2 *cups thinly sliced fresh mushrooms*

1 *cup finely chopped onions*
¼ *teaspoon salt*
¼ *teaspoon ground thyme*
¼ *teaspoon ground red pepper*

In a medium skillet over high heat, heat the oil until very hot. Add the okra and sauté, stirring, for 15 minutes, constantly scraping the bottom of the skillet with a wooden spoon. Add all the remaining ingredients and cook for 5 minutes, stirring often.

PER SERVING	KCAL	FATgm	CHOLmg	SODmg
	177	8	0	138

HOT AND SPICY BOILED OKRA

MAKES 2 SERVINGS

WHENEVER I prepare this recipe, it brings back memories of my dad. Okra was his favorite dish, and he liked it hot and spicy, just like this!

3 *cups water*
1 *pound small fresh okra*
⅛ *teaspoon salt*
½ *teaspoon ground black*
   pepper

1 *tablespoon tarragon*
   vinegar
½ *teaspoon hot pepper*
   sauce

In a medium saucepan over high heat, bring the water to a boil. Add the okra and reduce the heat to medium; cook for 10 minutes. Remove the okra with a slotted spoon and place on a warm serving plate. In a small bowl, combine all the remaining ingredients and mix well. sprinkle over the okra and serve.

PER SERVING	KCAL	FATgm	CHOLmg	SODmg
	73	0.4	0	150

PARSLIED ROAST POTATOES

MAKES 3 SERVINGS

POTATOES are a favorite among Cajun people. When Mama set the table for mealtime, you could bet there would be potatoes of some kind. I think the potato has been cooked every way imaginable, and this is one of my favorites!

¾ *pound small new*
 potatoes
½ *teaspoon vegetable*
 bouillon granules
1 *cup water*
½ *cup fresh pearl onions,*
 peeled

1 *tablespoon reduced-*
 calorie margarine
¼ *teaspoon salt*
⅛ *teaspoon ground black*
 pepper
2 *tablespoons very finely*
 chopped fresh parsley

Preheat the oven to 450°F.

Wash the potatoes and peel off a strip around the middle of each one. Dissolve the bouillon in the water. In a shallow baking pan, combine the potatoes, dissolved bouillon, onions, margarine, salt and black pepper. Cover with aluminum foil and bake for 30 minutes, turning the potatoes often to prevent burning.

Stir in the parsley and increase the oven temperature to 400°F. Bake, uncovered, for 20 minutes, or until the potatoes are golden brown, shaking the pan once or twice while baking.

PER SERVING	KCAL	FATgm	CHOLmg	SODmg
	125	2	0	219

ROSEMARY POTATOES

MAKES 4 SERVINGS

J ONE DAY I had a few small potatoes and some vegetable odds and ends. I cooked the potatoes in some stock, and then sautéed them with rosemary and green onions. What a delicious way to use up leftovers!

1 *pound small new potatoes*
3 *cups Chicken Stock (page 20) or water*
1 *small onion, quartered*
1 *rib celery, cut in half*
1 *carrot, cut into 3 pieces*

½ *small green bell pepper, cut in half*
1 *tablespoon olive oil*
1 *teaspoon rosemary leaves, crushed*
½ *cup chopped green onions*

In a large pot over high heat, combine the potatoes, chicken stock, onion, celery, carrot and bell pepper. Bring to a boil; reduce heat, cover, and cook for 30 minutes. Drain the potatoes, discarding the other vegetables.

In a small skillet over high heat, heat the olive oil until very hot. Add the potatoes, rosemary and green onions and sauté for 5 minutes, shaking the skillet constantly. Serve hot.

PER SERVING	KCAL	FATgm	CHOLmg	SODmg
	145	2	0	28

CAMP POTATOES

*J*YEARS AGO, when my children were growing up, one of our favorite pastimes was to go to some friends' camp to fish and ride on their houseboat. We loved cooking outdoors, and this potato dish was one of our favorites!

2 *tablespoons reduced-calorie margarine*

2 *large potatoes, peeled and cut into julienne*

1 *cup pearl onions, peeled*

1 *cup water*

2 *tablespoons dehydrated sweet bell pepper*

¼ *teaspoon ground turmeric*

¼ *teaspoon ground black pepper*

⅛ *teaspoon salt*

In a large skillet over high heat, melt the margarine until very hot. Add the potatoes and onions and sauté for 5 minutes or until brown, stirring constantly and scraping the bottom of the skillet with a wooden spoon. Add all the remaining ingredients, stirring well. Reduce the heat, cover, and simmer for 15 minutes, or until the potatoes are tender and all the liquid has evaporated.

PER SERVING	KCAL	FATgm	CHOLmg	SODmg
	133	4	0	186

MAMA HAZEL'S BAKED POTATOES

MAKES 4 SERVINGS

THIS IS PROBABLY the most unusual stuffed potato you'll ever prepare—and the most delicious.

4 medium baking
    potatoes, uncooked
¼ cup finely chopped
    green bell pepper
¼ cup finely chopped red
    bell pepper
½ teaspoon onion powder
½ teaspoon garlic powder

¼ teaspoon salt
⅛ teaspoon dried oregano
    leaves, crushed
⅛ teaspoon ground red
    pepper
Paprika
2 teaspoons reduced-
    calorie margarine

Preheat the oven to 375°F.

Peel the potatoes and scoop out the centers with a spoon, leaving a shell about ¼ inch thick. Finely chop the potato pulp and mix with the bell peppers, onion powder, garlic powder, salt, oregano and red pepper; mix well and spoon back into the potato shells. Sprinkle each potato with paprika and dot with ½ teaspoon of the margarine. Place the potatoes in a baking pan that has been sprayed with nonstick vegetable cooking spray. Pour about ¾ cup water into the bottom, cover with aluminum foil and bake for 30 minutes, or until the potato shells are tender. Uncover and cook an additional 20 minutes, or until the potatoes are light brown.

PER SERVING	KCAL	FATgm	CHOLmg	SODmg
	163	1	0	156

SCOTTY'S TURNIP AND POTATO CASSEROLE

MAKES 3 SERVINGS

*J*MY MOM AND DAD grew turnips in their garden. Although it was their favorite, some of us complained of a strong aftertaste, so Mom cooked them with potatoes to give them a milder taste. My grandson Scotty helped me create this low-calorie version, so I named it in his honor.

1 *quart water*
1 *medium turnip, peeled and chopped*
1 *medium potato, peeled and chopped*
1 *medium onion, chopped*
⅓ *cup chopped green bell pepper*
⅓ *cup chopped yellow bell pepper*

⅓ *cup chopped red bell pepper*
⅛ *teaspoon ground red pepper*
⅛ *teaspoon ground black pepper*
½ *cup turnip-potato liquid*
½ *cup evaporated skim milk*

Preheat the over to 350°F.

In a 2-quart pot over high heat, bring the water to a boil. Add the turnip and potato; reduce the heat to medium and cook for about 8 minutes, or until tender. Remove from the heat, drain the vegetables, and set aside. Reserve ½ cup turnip-potato cooking liquid.

Spray the inside of a medium skillet with nonstick vegetable cooking spray and place over medium heat. Add the onion, green, yellow and bell peppers, and red and black pepper. Cook, stirring, for 8 minutes, or until the onion mixture starts to stick. Add the stock and milk and continue cooking for 1 minute. Remove from the heat.

Spray the inside of a 1-quart casserole dish with nonstick vegetable cooking spray. Combine both mixtures in the casserole, cover and bake for 25 minutes. Serve hot.

PER SERVING	KCAL	FATgm	CHOLmg	SODmg
	116	0.5	2	90

MAMA HAZEL'S WHITE SQUASH

MAKES 2 CUPS

WHITE SQUASH, also known as pattypan squash, is a favorite in Cajun country, and this recipe has just a touch of sweetness.

4 medium white squash,
    peeled and thinly
    sliced (about 7 cups)
3 cups water
½ cup sugar

1 tablespoon reduced-
    calorie margarine
1 teaspoon vanilla extract
½ teaspoon ground
    nutmeg

In a large saucepan over high heat, combine the squash and water and boil, uncovered, for 10 minutes, stirring often. Add all the remaining ingredients and continue to cook, stirring often, until the squash is tender and the liquid has evaporated, about 20 minutes.

PER SERVING	KCAL	FATgm	CHOLmg	SODmg
	274	4	0	91

CORN MAQUE CHOUX

MAKES 3 SERVINGS

*J*WE CAN'T WAIT till the fresh sweet corn is ready to pick. If you like corn, you will love this sweet, yet highly seasoned, corn dish. Serve it as a side dish or add some sautéed crawfish tails or shrimp to the maque choux (pronounced mock-*shoe*) for a hearty main dish.

You can use frozen corn as well.

6 *ears fresh corn, cut from the cob (about 2½ cups)*
1 *tablespoon reduced-calorie margarine*
1 *cup chopped onions*
⅓ *cup finely chopped green bell pepper*

⅛ *teaspoon salt*
⅛ *teaspoon ground red pepper*
3 *tablespoons sugar*
½ *cup evaporated skim milk*

In a medium saucepan over medium heat, combine the corn, margarine, onions, bell pepper, salt and red pepper; cook for 5 minutes, stirring constantly. Add the sugar and milk and cook for 10 minutes, or until the corn is tender.

PER SERVING	KCAL	FATgm	CHOLmg	SODmg
	284	4	2	204

CREAMED CABBAGE

MAKES 6 SERVINGS

THIS RECIPE is easy to prepare, makes a great side dish and tastes fantastic!

1 *small head cabbage, coarsely chopped (about 6 cups)*
2 *tablespoons reduced-calorie margarine*
1 *cup finely chopped onions*
½ *cup finely chopped green bell pepper*
⅓ *cup finely chopped celery*
One *10½-ounce can reduced-calorie cream of mushroom soup*

1 *cup evaporated skim milk*
½ *teaspoon salt*
½ *teaspoon ground white pepper*
½ *teaspoon minced fresh garlic*
⅛ *teaspoon paprika*
⅛ *teaspoon coarsely ground black pepper*

Preheat the oven to 350°F.

Place the cabbage in a large bowl and add enough water to cover; let soak for a few minutes to clean the cabbage, then drain and place in an 1½-quart baking dish that has been sprayed with nonstick vegetable cooking spray; set aside.

In a medium saucepan over high heat, melt the margarine and add the onions, bell pepper, and celery. Cook, stirring, for 5 minutes. Add the next 5 ingredients and cook for 5 minutes, stirring often. Remove from the heat and pour over the cabbage. Sprinkle with the paprika and black pepper. Bake for 30 minutes.

PER SERVING	KCAL	FATgm	CHOLmg	SODmg
	92	2	2	198

BAKED STUFFED MIRLITON

MAKES 6 SERVINGS

IN SOUTH LOUISIANA we call the pear-shaped squash known as the vegetable pear or chayote a mirliton (pronounced *mel-uh-ton*, with just a hint of the *n* at the end.)

3 medium mirlitons (page 14), peeled and cut in half
1 tablespoon reduced-calorie margarine
½ pound medium shrimp, peeled, deveined and coarsely chopped
½ teaspoon salt
½ teaspoon granulated garlic
1 teaspoon paprika
⅛ teaspoon ground oregano
⅛ teaspoon ground thyme
⅛ teaspoon ground red pepper
⅛ teaspoon ground black pepper
⅓ cup evaporated skim milk
⅓ cup chopped green onions
1 tablespoon dehydrated onion
½ cup plus 6 tablespoons fine dry bread crumbs
1 cup seafood stock or water

Preheat the oven to 350°F. Spray an 8-inch-square baking dish with nonstick vegetable cooking spray and set aside.

Place the mirlitons in a large pot or Dutch oven. Cover the mirlitons with water; boil for 30 minutes, or until tender when pierced with a fork. Remove from the heat, drain and set aside to cool.

Using a small spoon, scoop out the center of each mirliton, and remove the seed, leaving a ½-inch shell all around. Put the pulp in a separate bowl. Chop the mirliton pulp and set aside. (You should have about 2 cups.)

In a large skillet over medium heat, melt the margarine. Add the shrimp, salt, garlic, paprika, oregano, thyme and red and black peppers. Cook for 5 minutes, stirring often. Add reserved mirliton pulp, milk, green onion, dehydrated onion, and ½ cup of the bread crumbs. Cook an additional 5 minutes, stirring often to mix well. Remove the skillet from the heat and spoon equal amounts of the shrimp mixture into each shell, topping each shell with 1 tablespoon bread crumbs.

Arrange the stuffed mirlitons in the prepared dish and spray each one with cooking spray. Add seafood stock or water to baking dish. Bake, uncovered, for 30 minutes. Serve hot.

PER SERVING	KCAL	FATgm	CHOLmg	SODmg
	69	2	74	143

MIRLITON AU GRATIN

THIS DISH has a very rich and creamy sauce. The key ingredient is the evaporated skim milk. You can create a sauce so wonderful using skim milk, you'll have a hard time convincing others it's low-calorie!

3 *medium mirlitons*
2 *tablespoons reduced-*
   calorie margarine
1 *cup fresh pearl onions,*
   peeled
½ *teaspoon salt*
¼ *teaspoon ground white*
   pepper

1 *cup evaporated skim*
   milk
1 *tablespoon Roux Flour*
   (page 18)
½ *teaspoon paprika*

Preheat the oven to 350°F.

Peel the mirlitons and cut them in half lengthwise. Remove the seed from the center, then cut them into julienne.

In a medium skillet over high heat, melt the margarine. Add the mirliton, onions, salt and white pepper; cook for 15 minutes, stirring constantly. Remove from heat and transfer to a 2-quart casserole dish that has been sprayed with nonstick vegetable cooking spray; set aside.

In same skillet over high heat, heat the milk until very hot and add the roux flour. Cook, stirring constantly, for 15 minutes, or until the sauce thickens. Remove from the heat and pour over the mirliton mixture, then sprinkle with the paprika. Bake for 30 minutes.

PER SERVING	KCAL	FATgm	CHOLmg	SODmg
	142	7	3	271

ORANGE CARROTS

MAKES 2 SERVINGS

2 *large carrots, cut into*
  ½-inch-thick slices
  (about 1½ cups)
One 6-ounce can
  unsweetened orange
  juice

1 *tablespoon brown sugar*
  substitute
¼ *teaspoon finely*
  shredded orange peel
⅛ *teaspoon minced*
  crystallized ginger

In a small saucepan over high heat, bring 1 cup water to a boil; add the carrots and boil for 5 minutes. Drain and set aside.

In the same saucepan, combine the orange juice, brown sugar substitute, orange peel and ginger. Place over low heat; and cook, stirring for 10 minutes, or until the sauce thickens. Add the carrots and cook for 5 minutes longer.

PER SERVING	KCAL	FATgm	CHOLmg	SODmg
	69	0.3	0	29

MUSTARD GREENS

MAKES 2 SERVINGS

*M*USTARD GREENS always grew in our garden. We had to wash the leaves repeatedly to get all the dirt off, but that's about the only thing I didn't like about mustard greens—because the taste is fantastic!

2 *bunches (10 ounces
    each) mustard greens*
¼ *cup water*
½ *cup finely chopped
    onions*
½ *teaspoon minced garlic*

⅛ *teaspoon salt*
⅛ *teaspoon ground white
    pepper*
⅛ *teaspoon ground thyme*
⅛ *teaspoon dried basil
    leaves, crushed*

In a large saucepan over high heat, bring 2 quarts of water and the mustard greens to a boil. Boil for 20 minutes, or until the greens are tender. Remove from heat, drain and set aside.

Spray the inside of a large skillet with nonstick vegetable cooking spray and place over medium heat. Add the drained greens, water and onions; cook for 5 minutes, stirring often. Stir in all the remaining ingredients. Cook, stirring, for 20 minutes longer, or until all the liquid has evaporated. Serve hot.

PER SERVING	KCAL	FATgm	CHOLmg	SODmg
	58	.80	0	182

ASPARAGUS A LA TONI

MAKES 3 SERVINGS

MY DAUGHTER TONI loves asparagus, so I made this tasty treat for her!

½ *pound fresh asparagus spears, trimmed*
1 *medium tomato, peeled, seeded and quartered*
2 *tablespoons low-fat cottage cheese*

1 *teaspoon balsamic vinegar*
½ *teaspoon dried basil leaves, crushed*
¼ *teaspoon salt*

In a 4-quart saucepan over high heat, bring 2 cups of water to a boil. Add the asparagus and cook for 2 to 3 minutes for crisp-tender, or to desired doneness. Drain and place on a serving plate.

Combine the tomato, cottage cheese, vinegar, basil and salt in a food processor or blender and process until smooth. Pour into a medium saucepan over high heat and bring to a boil. Reduce the heat and simmer, stirring, for 5 minutes, or until the sauce thickens. Remove from the heat and spoon over asparagus.

PER SERVING	KCAL	FATgm	CHOLmg	SODmg
	34	0.4	0.4	213

EGGPLANT ROUNDS

MAKES 4 SERVINGS

THESE LIGHT AND CRISPY ROUNDS will be the perfect appetizer for your next party.

¼ *teaspoon salt*
½ *teaspoon paprika*
¼ *teaspoon ground white*
  pepper
¼ *teaspoon ground*
  oregano

½ *large eggplant, peeled*
  and sliced into
  ⅛-inch rounds
⅓ *cup evaporated skim*
  milk
½ *cup dry bread crumbs*

In a small bowl, combine the salt, paprika, white pepper and oregano; mix well and sprinkle on both sides of the eggplant slices. Dip the seasoned eggplant in the milk, then dredge in the bread crumbs.

Spray the inside of a large baking pan with nonstick vegetable cooking spray. Place the eggplant in the pan and spray each slice with the cooking spray. Broil 5 to 6 inches from the heat for 7 minutes, or until golden brown; turn the slices over and broil for 7 minutes longer, or until golden brown and crisp.

PER SERVING	KCAL	FATgm	CHOLmg	SODmg
	87	2	1	241

BROCCOLI WITH MUSHROOM-WINE SAUCE

MAKES 2 SERVINGS

2 *cups fresh broccoli florets*

1 *cup low-fat cottage cheese*

1 *tablespoon reduced-calorie margarine*

3 *thinly sliced onion rings*

3 *thinly sliced green bell pepper rings*

½ *cup red wine*

¼ *teaspoon dried basil leaves, crushed*

⅛ *teaspoon ground white pepper*

2 *cups sliced fresh mushrooms*

½ *cup Chicken Stock (page 20) or water*

1 *teaspoon finely chopped fresh parsley*

1 *tablespoon grated Parmesan cheese*

Drop the broccoli into a pot of boiling water for 30 seconds; drain and set aside. Place the cottage cheese in a blender and process until smooth; set aside.

In a medium skillet over medium heat, melt the margarine. Add the onion and bell pepper rings and cook for 1 minute. Stir in ⅓ cup of the blended cottage cheese. (Refrigerate the remaining cottage cheese for another use.) Add the wine, basil and white pepper; cook for 10 minutes, stirring often. Add the mushrooms, stock and broccoli. Cook for 10 minutes longer, then stir in the parsley. Remove from the heat and sprinkle with the cheese.

PER SERVING	KCAL	FATgm	CHOLmg	SODmg
	194	2	4	315

SWEET POTATOES WITH ORANGE

MAKES 3 SERVINGS

WHEN BAKED, the combination of ingredients blends to make this dish unforgettable.

1 *pound fresh sweet*
  potatoes
¼ *cup sugar*
¼ *teaspoon ground*
  nutmeg

¼ *teaspoon ground*
  cinnamon
1 *medium orange, peeled*
  and halved

Preheat the oven to 425°F.

Scrub the sweet potatoes and bake for 45 minutes to 1 hour, or until tender. Allow them to cool to the touch; peel and cut into ½-inch slices. Reduce the oven to 350°F.

Spray the inside of a 9-by-5-by-3-inch loaf pan with nonstick vegetable cooking spray. Arrange *half* the potato slices in the pan, overlapping them slightly. Combine the sugar, nutmeg and cinnamon and sprinkle *half* over the potatoes. Cut 1 of the orange halves into thin slices and arrange on top of the potatoes. Follow with another layer of potatoes and sprinkle with the remaining sugar mixture. Squeeze the juice from remaining orange half over the top of the potatoes and spray with nonstick vegetable cooking spray. Cover with aluminum foil and bake for 15 minutes; remove the foil and turn the potatoes in the pan. Cover and bake for an additional 15 minutes. Cut into squares and serve hot.

PER SERVING	KCAL	FATgm	CHOLmg	SODmg
	239	0.3	0	16

CANDIED YAMS

MAKES 4 SERVINGS

WHEN COOKED, this dish is thick and rich like hot candy. In fact, some people say it's good enough to be dessert!

4 medium yams, baked, peeled and cut into ½-inch slices
¼ cup water
½ teaspoon brown sugar substitute
⅛ teaspoon imitation butter flavoring
⅛ teaspoon imitation vanilla and butter-nut flavoring
2 tablespoons pecan meal
10 miniature marshmallows

Preheat the oven to 350°F.

Arrange the potato slices in an 8-inch-square baking dish that has been sprayed with nonstick vegetable cooking spray; set aside. In a small bowl, combine the water, brown sugar substitute, and flavorings; mix well and pour over the potatoes. Sprinkle with the pecan meal, then top with the marshmallows. Bake for 15 minutes.

PER SERVING	KCAL	FATgm	CHOLmg	SODmg
	144	2	0	12

WATERMELON RIND PRESERVES

MAKES 4 CUPS

MOM CANNED a sweeter version of these, and we ate them on hot homemade bread. These, too, are good on bread, or if you can afford the calories, try them on a thin slice of angel food cake.

7 cups watermelon rind, with a small amount of red left on it (about ½ watermelon)
2 cups water
1 tablespoon brown sugar substitute
½ teaspoon cornstarch

1 tablespoon warm water
½ cup sugar
½ teaspoon balsamic vinegar
½ teaspoon imitation butter flavoring
½ teaspoon vanilla extract

Peel off green skin from the watermelon rind and cut the rind into ½-inch cubes. In a large pot, over medium heat combine the water and brown sugar substitute and cook for 40 minutes, stirring often. Dissolve the cornstarch in the warm water and stir into the watermelon along with remaining ingredients. Simmer, covered, for 30 minutes, stirring occasionally. Pour into two 2-pint sterilized jars and cover tightly. Store in refrigerator up to 3 weeks.

PER CUP	KCAL	FATgm	CHOLmg	SODmg
	139	0.06	0	19

RICE, DRESSINGS

RICE

AND OTHER

SIDE DISHES

BASIC WHITE RICE

MAKES 4 CUPS

2 *cups water*
2 *cups converted rice*

Combine the water and rice in a 2-quart saucepan. Cover and bring to a boil over medium heat; cook for 10 minutes. Reduce the heat to a simmer; simmer for 5 minutes longer. Serve hot.

PER ½-CUP SERVING	KCAL	FATgm	CHOLmg	SODmg
	171	0.3	0	1

LOUISIANA GREEN RICE

MAKES 4 SERVINGS

THIS DISH has a hearty flavor and it's great anytime.

2 *cups Chicken Stock (page 20) or water*
1 *cup uncooked rice*
½ *cup chopped green bell pepper*
⅓ *cup chopped fresh jalapeño peppers*

3 *tablespoons chopped fresh parsley*
1 *teaspoon reduced-calorie margarine*
¼ *teaspoon salt*
1 *bay leaf*

Preheat the oven to 350°F.

Spray the inside of a 1½-quart baking dish with nonstick vegetable cooking spray. Combine all the ingredients and mix well. Bake, covered for 30 minutes, stirring once halfway through the cooking time. Remove the bay leaf before serving.

PER SERVING	KCAL	FATgm	CHOLmg	SODmg
	177	1	0	222

DIRTY RICE

MAKES 3 CUPS

A FAMOUS Louisiana side dish. Serve it with baked or bar-becued chicken.

1 cup water
½ pound chicken livers
    (1 cup)
1 cup chopped onions
½ cup finely chopped
    green bell pepper
½ cup finely chopped
    celery
½ pound ground round or
    chuck
½ teaspoon salt
½ teaspoon browning and
    seasoning sauce

¼ teaspoon ground red
    pepper
¼ teaspoon ground black
    pepper
1½ cups Chicken Stock
    (page 20) or water
½ cup finely chopped
    green onions
3 tablespoons finely
    chopped fresh
    parsley
2 cups hot cooked rice

In a 1-quart saucepan over high heat, bring the water to a boil. Add the chicken livers and boil for 5 minutes; drain and reserve the liquid. Let the livers cool to the touch, then chop finely and set aside.

Spray the inside of a 4-quart pot with nonstick vegetable cook-ing spray and place over high heat. Add the onions, bell pepper and celery. Sauté for 10 minutes, stirring constantly to prevent burning. Add the livers, ground round or chuck, and the next 4 ingredients. Continue cooking for about 15 minutes, or until the meat browns, stirring often. Add the chicken stock and the re-served liver stock and cook for 5 minutes longer.

Remove from the heat and stir in the green onions, parsley and rice; mix well. Cover and let stand for 10 minutes, allowing the rice to absorb the liquid and meat flavor.

PER SERVING	KCAL	FATgm	CHOLmg	SODmg
	183	4	178	215

PECAN RICE

MAKES THREE 1-CUP SERVINGS

THIS DISH is delicious as is, or you can add some sautéed fresh shrimp for a main meal dish.

½ *cup finely chopped*
  onions
2 *tablespoons finely*
  chopped celery
2 *tablespoons pecan*
  meal
2 *cups water*
1 *cup quick-cooking (not*
  instant) rice

1 *tablespoon butter-*
  flavored sprinkles
¼ *teaspoon salt*
½ *teaspoon ground red*
  pepper
½ *teaspoon chili powder*

Spray the inside of a small skillet with nonstick vegetable cooking spray and place over high heat. Add the onions, celery and pecan meal; sauté, stirring, for 3 minutes, then remove from the heat and set aside.

In a medium saucepan over medium heat, add the water, rice, onion mixture and all the remaining ingredients, stirring well. Cook, covered, for 30 minutes, or until the rice is tender.

PER SERVING	KCAL	FATgm	CHOLmg	SODmg
	196	1	0	196

BROCCOLI-CHEESE RICE

MAKES FOUR 1-CUP SERVINGS

THE CHEFS in my kitchen prepare this dish often. My son, Sonny, won a ribbon at the International Rice Festival, held every October in Crowley, Louisiana, with this dish. Of course I reduced the calories in this version, but not the taste!

2 cups water
2 cups fresh broccoli
    florets
1 tablespoon salt-free
    chicken bouillon
    granules
One-half 10½-ounce can
    reduced-calorie cream
    of mushroom soup
1 cup quick-cooking (not
    instant) rice

⅓ cup shredded reduced-
    fat Cheddar cheese
1 tablespoon minced fresh
    onion
1 tablespoon dehydrated
    sweet bell pepper
1 teaspoon ground red
    pepper

In a medium saucepan over high heat, bring *1* cup of the water to a boil. Add the broccoli and boil for 5 minutes; drain and allow to cool to the touch, then chop fine.

In same saucepan over medium heat, combine the remaining 1 cup water, the chopped broccoli, and all the remaining ingredients. Cook, covered, for 30 minutes, or until the rice is tender, stirring often.

PER SERVING	KCAL	FATgm	CHOLmg	SODmg
	216	2	5	210

CHEESY RICE PILAF

MAKES 4 SERVINGS

THIS PILAF goes well with any fish, meat or poultry dish.

2 *teaspoons reduced-calorie margarine*
½ *cup finely chopped green onions*
2 *tablespoons finely chopped green bell pepper*

2 *tablespoons finely chopped red bell pepper*
2 *cups cooked rice*
2 *tablespoons shredded reduced-fat Cheddar cheese*

In a large skillet over medium heat, melt the margarine. Add the green onions and green and red bell peppers and cook for 3 minutes, stirring often. Reduce the heat to low and stir in the rice and cheese. Cook for 2 minutes, or until the rice is hot and the cheese is melted, stirring often.

PER SERVING	KCAL	FATgm	CHOLmg	SODmg
	120	2	0	104

VEGETABLE-AND-RICE RING MOLD

MAKES 8 SERVINGS

A BEAUTIFUL PRESENTATION for rice and vegetables.

1 *tablespoon cornstarch*
1½ *cups evaporated skim milk*
2½ *cups cooked rice*
1 *cup finely shredded carrots*
½ *cup very finely chopped onions*
One 5-ounce package frozen peas, thawed
1 *egg, beaten*

1 *tablespoon low-sodium Worcestershire sauce*
½ *teaspoon hot pepper sauce*
½ *teaspoon salt*
½ *teaspoon ground white pepper*
Lemon slices
Parsley sprigs

Preheat the oven to 350°F.

In a large bowl, dissolve the cornstarch in the milk, then add all the remaining ingredients. Stir until well mixed and pour into a 9-inch fluted tube pan that has been sprayed with nonstick vegetable cooking spray. Cover the pan with aluminum foil and place in a water bath (a large baking dish filled about halfway with water). Bake for 1 hour. Remove from oven and let cool at least 1 hour, then loosen the edges of the ring with a spatula. Transfer the mold to a large round serving platter and garnish with lemon slices and fresh parsley.

PER SERVING	KCAL	FATgm	CHOLmg	SODmg
	120	1	36	201

TURKEY-RICE-EGGPLANT DRESSING

MAKES 6 SERVINGS

1 tablespoon reduced-calorie margarine

1½ pounds ground turkey

1 large eggplant, peeled and diced

1 cup finely chopped onions

⅓ cup finely chopped green bell pepper

⅓ cup finely chopped celery

1 tablespoon low-sodium Worcestershire sauce

½ teaspoon salt

½ teaspoon ground red pepper

½ teaspoon ground black pepper

½ teaspoon browning and seasoning sauce

½ cup Chicken Stock (page 20) or water

2 cups hot cooked rice

⅓ cup finely chopped green onions

1 tablespoon finely chopped fresh parsley

In a medium saucepan over high heat, melt the margarine. Add the turkey, and cook, stirring, for 10 minutes, or until brown. Add the eggplant, onions, bell pepper, celery, Worcestershire salt, red and black peppers, and browning and seasoning sauce, mixing well after each addition. Reduce the heat to medium, cover, and simmer for 20 minutes, stirring often. Add the stock, rice, green onions and parsley and cook for 3 minutes, stirring occasionally. Remove from the heat and let stand a few minutes before serving.

PER SERVING	KCAL	FATgm	CHOLmg	SODmg
	255	3	0.2	241

TURKEY-CORNBREAD DRESSING

MAKES 8 SERVINGS

1 *pound ground turkey*
One *¼-ounce envelope*
    instant mushroom-onion
    soup mix
3 *cups water*
½ *teaspoon ground white*
    pepper
½ *teaspoon ground red*
    pepper
1 *egg plus 2 egg whites*
½ *cup evaporated skim*
    milk

2 *slices bread (40 calories*
    per slice), cut into
    ¼-inch cubes
2 *cups Jalapeño*
    Cornbread, crumbled
    (page 233)
½ *cup finely chopped*
    green onions
½ *teaspoon paprika*

Preheat the oven to 350F.

Spray the inside of a large skillet with nonstick vegetable cooking spray and place over high heat. Add the turkey and sauté, stirring for 10 minutes, or until brown. Add the soup mix, water and white and red pepper; cook, stirring, for 15 minutes, then remove from the heat.

In a small bowl, beat the egg and egg whites into the milk and slowly add to skillet. Set aside.

Spray the inside of an 8-inch-square baking dish with nonstick vegetable cooking spray. Spoon the turkey mixture into the dish, then add the bread cubes, mashing them with the back of a spoon to absorb the liquid. Mix in the cornbread and green onions, then sprinkle with paprika. Bake for 20 minutes.

PER SERVING	KCAL	FATgm	CHOLmg	SODmg
	130	1	83	175

SAUCES AND

GRAVIES

ONION-MUSHROOM SAUCE

MAKES 1 CUP

SERVE THIS SAUCE over rice or on baked potatoes.

1 *tablespoon vegetable oil*
2 *tablespoons sugar*
1 *cup finely chopped onions*
1 *cup finely chopped fresh mushrooms*
1 *cup Chicken Stock (page 20) or water*
1 *tablespoon Roux Flour (page 18)*
2 *teaspoons balsamic vinegar*

¼ *teaspoon salt*
½ *teaspoon paprika*
¼ *teaspoon ground white pepper*
¼ *teaspoon ground oregano*
2 *tablespoons very finely chopped green onions*
1 *tablespoon very finely chopped fresh parsley*

In a medium skillet over high heat, heat the oil until very hot. Add the sugar and cook, stirring, for 1 minute, or until the sugar turns dark brown. Add the next 9 ingredients; stir until well mixed and cook for 10 minutes, stirring often. Add the green onions and parsley; cook an additional 10 minutes.

PER TABLESPOON	KCAL	FATgm	CHOLmg	SODmg
	15	1	0	37

MUSHROOM-WINE SAUCE

MAKES 2 SERVINGS

SERVE THIS SAUCE with fish or grilled chicken.

1 *cup low-fat cottage cheese*
1 *tablespoon reduced-calorie margarine*
3 *thinly sliced onion rings*
3 *thinly sliced green bell pepper rings*
½ *cup red wine*
¼ *teaspoon dried basil leaves, crushed*

⅛ *teaspoon ground white pepper*
2 *cups thinly sliced mushrooms*
½ *cup Chicken Stock (page 20) or water*
1 *teaspoon finely chopped fresh parsley*

Place the cottage cheese in a blender and process until smooth; set aside.

In a small skillet over medium heat, melt the margarine. Add the onion and bell pepper rings and cook for 1 minute, stirring often. Add 2 *tablespoons* of the blended cottage cheese (refrigerate the remaining cottage cheese for another use), the wine, basil and white pepper. Cook, uncovered, for 10 minutes, stirring often. Add the mushrooms and stock and cook for 10 minutes. Stir in the parsley and remove from the heat. Serve immediately.

PER SERVING	KCAL	FATgm	CHOLmg	SODmg
	113	3	0.5	174

MUSTARD SAUCE

MAKES 1 CUP

WE SERVE a higher-calorie version of this with pan-fried rabbit at the Cajun Cafe.

¼ cup evaporated skim
   milk
3 ounces plain low-fat
   yogurt

2 teaspoons Creole
   mustard
2 tablespoons reduced-
   calorie mayonnaise

In a small saucepan over high heat, combine the milk, yogurt and mustard and bring to a boil. Reduce the heat to medium; cook, stirring, for 1 minute, or until the sauce thickens. Remove from the heat and stir in mayonnaise. Serve hot.

PER TABLESPOON	KCAL	FATgm	CHOLmg	SODmg
	13	1	1	34

COLD MUSTARD SAUCE

MAKES 1 CUP

THIS SAUCE makes a great dip for fresh vegetables, or it can be served with fish, chicken or meat.

2 *tablespoons prepared mustard*
1 *tablespoon cider vinegar*
1 *tablespoon sugar*

3 *tablespoons vegetable oil*
¼ *cup evaporated skim milk*
2 *teaspoons very finely chopped fresh dill-weed*

In a small bowl, combine the mustard, vinegar and sugar. Beat vigorously while adding a little oil at a time; the sauce will thicken rapidly. Stir in the milk and dill weed. Chill before serving.

PER TABLESPOON	KCAL	FATgm	CHOLmg	SODmg
	31	3	0.1	29

HOMEMADE TOMATO SAUCE

MAKES 5 CUPS

6 *medium tomatoes,*
  peeled, seeded and
  chopped (about 3
  cups)
One-half 6-ounce can
  tomato paste
2 *cups salt-free tomato*
  juice

1 *cup water*
¼ *cup white vinegar*
1 *teaspoon ground sage*
1 *teaspoon ground thyme*
1 *teaspoon ground*
  oregano
¼ *teaspoon salt*

In a large saucepan over medium heat, combine all ingredients and cook for 30 minutes, stirring often. Transfer to a food processor or blender and process till pureed.

Pour the mixture through a strainer, discarding the remains. Return the strained mixture to the same saucepan over medium heat; cook for 20 minutes, or until the sauce thickens.

PER CUP	KCAL	FATgm	CHOLmg	SODmg
	92	1	0	156

HOMEMADE BARBECUE SAUCE

MAKES 4 CUPS

2 *tablespoons vegetable oil*
2 *cups finely chopped onions*
½ *cup finely chopped green bell pepper*
½ *cup finely chopped celery*
3 *cups water*
One-half 6-ounce can *tomato paste*

½ *cup low-sodium catsup*
3 *tablespoons low-sodium Worcestershire sauce*
2 *tablespoons low-sodium prepared mustard*
1 *teaspoon liquid smoke*
1 *teaspoon hot pepper sauce*
1 *teaspoon salt*
1 *teaspoon brown sugar substitute*

In a medium saucepan over high heat, heat the oil until very hot. Add the onions, bell pepper and celery and cook for 10 minutes, stirring often. Reduce the heat to medium and add the next 9 ingredients, stirring well. Cook, covered, for 20 minutes. Reduce the heat and simmer, covered, for 15 minutes, stirring occasionally.

PER CUP	KCAL	FATgm	CHOLmg	SODmg
	166	8	0	381

PRUDHOMME'S CAJUN COCKTAIL SAUCE

MAKES ¾ CUP

THIS SPICY SAUCE is great with shrimp or crab, but with boiled crawfish it can't be beat!

3 *tablespoons tomato paste*
3 *tablespoons white wine*
1 *tablespoon reduced-calorie mayonnaise*
1 *tablespoon catsup*
2 *teaspoons honey*

2 *teaspoons prepared horseradish*
½ *teaspoon chili powder*
½ *teaspoon hot pepper sauce*
¼ *teaspoon minced fresh garlic*

Combine all the ingredients in a blender; cover and blend on medium speed for about 1 minute, or until smooth. Chill for at least 1 hour before serving.

PER TABLESPOON	KCAL	FATgm	CHOLmg	SODmg
	22	0.44	0.5	26

TARTAR SAUCE

MAKES ABOUT 1¼ CUPS

AT LAST, a low-calorie tartar sauce!

1 *cup low-fat cottage cheese*
¼ *cup reduced-calorie mayonnaise*
2 *tablespoons very finely chopped sweet pickle*
2 *tablespoons very finely chopped onions*

1 *teaspoon low-sodium Worcestershire sauce*
⅛ *teaspoon ground red pepper*
⅛ *teaspoon ground black pepper*

Place the cottage cheese in a blender and process until smooth; put *half* in a small bowl. (Refrigerate the remaining cottage cheese for another use.) Stir in all the remaining ingredients and mix well. Cover and refrigerate at least for 1 hour before serving.

PER TABLESPOON	KCAL	FATgm	CHOLmg	SODmg
	28	2	3	66

CREAMY CHICKEN GRAVY

MAKES 2 CUPS

SERVE THIS DISH with Southern-Style Oven-Fried Chicken
(page 127), or use it as a topping on potatoes or vegetables.

2 *tablespoons quick-*
   mixing flour
¼ *cup evaporated skim*
   milk
½ *teaspoon very finely*
   chopped onions

1 *cup Chicken Stock*
   (page 20) or *water*
¼ *teaspoon ground white*
   pepper

In a small bowl, combine the flour and milk and stir until
smooth; set aside.

In a small saucepan over high heat, combine the onions and
stock and bring to a boil. Slowly stir in the milk mixture. Reduce
the heat, add white pepper and simmer, stirring, for 5 minutes,
or until the sauce thickens. Serve hot.

PER TABLESPOON	KCAL	FATgm	CHOLmg	SODmg
	5	0.01	0.1	3

BREADS AND MUFFINS

IKE'S LIGHT LOAF BREAD

MAKES ONE 9-BY-5-LOAF, OR 10 SERVINGS

MY SON-IN-LAW and chef, Ike Broussard, says, "I never tire of the aroma of fresh homemade bread baking. It was a real challenge to bake bread that was low in calories, yet tasted as good as regular bread. I bet you can't tell the difference!"

*2 cups hot water (about
   105°F)*
*Two ¼-ounce packets dry
   yeast*
*¼ cup reduced-calorie
   margarine, melted*

6 cups all-purpose flour
1 tablespoon sugar
1½ teaspoons salt

In a medium bowl, combine the water, yeast and margarine. Whisk together with a wire whisk, then let stand for 5 minutes.

In a large bowl, combine the flour, sugar and salt. Add *half* the liquid yeast mixture, mixing well. Add the remaining liquid and mix until the flour is thoroughly incorporated. With floured hands, place the dough onto a lightly floured surface and knead by hand until the dough is smooth and slightly sticky to the touch.

Place the dough in a large bowl that has been sprayed with nonstick vegetable cooking spray. Spray the top of the dough with the cooking spray and cover with a clean, dry towel; let stand in a warm place until the dough doubles in size.

Remove the towel, and with your fist, punch the dough down, then place it on a lightly floured surface. Shape the dough into a loaf by pressing down and rolling with the palm of your hand and your fingertips, tucking in the sides while rolling. Spray a 9-by-5-by-3-inch loaf pan with nonstick vegetable cooking spray. Put the dough in the pan and cover with the dry towel; allow the dough to rise until double in size again.

Preheat the oven to 325°F. Remove the towel and bake the bread for 45 minutes, or until golden brown on top. Let the bread cool for 15 minutes before serving.

PER SERVING	KCAL	FATgm	CHOLmg	SODmg
	230	3	0	347

CAJUN COUCHE-COUCHE

MAKES 2 SERVINGS

COUCHE-COUCHE is fried corn dough, and when I was a child, we ate it frequently for breakfast with fresh cow's milk. I always liked to eat mine with some of Mama's canned figs or cane syrup. This old-time recipe is still a favorite of mine, especially this low-calorie version. Leftover couche-couche can also be used for cornbread dressing or stuffing.

1 *cup yellow cornmeal*
½ *teaspoon baking*
powder
¼ *teaspoon salt*

1 *tablespoon reduced-*
calorie margarine
1 *cup water*
Milk

In a small bowl, combine the cornmeal, baking powder, and salt. In medium cast-iron skillet over high heat, melt the margarine until very hot.

While heating the skillet, stir ½ cup of the water into the cornmeal (the mixture will be lumpy). Pour the cornmeal mixture into the skillet and cook for 5 minutes, stirring constantly. While stirring, gradually add the remaining water to the skillet. Cook, stirring for 10 minutes, or until the cornmeal is no longer lumpy. The finished couche-couche will be moist.

Remove from the heat and serve immediately in bowls with milk, and fruit if desired, on top.

PER SERVING	KCAL	FATgm	CHOLmg	SODmg
	228	4	0	519

SWEET POTATO MUFFINS

MAKES 18 MUFFINS

*J*IKE BROUSSARD is married to my oldest daughter, Diane, and he is one of our chefs at Prudhomme's Cajun Cafe. His sweeter version of this recipe is served at the café and has become very popular. In fact, his original recipe appeared in *Gourmet* magazine. Because these muffins are so popular, Ike created a low-calorie version for this cookbook that is just as good!

1 *medium sweet potato, peeled and grated (¾ cup)*	1 *teaspoon ground cinnamon*
1 *cup all-purpose flour*	¼ *teaspoon ground nutmeg*
½ *cup sugar*	*Dash of salt*
¼ *cup raisins*	1 *cup skim milk*
¼ *cup chopped pecans or walnuts (optional)*	¼ *cup reduced-calorie margarine, melted*
1½ *teaspoons baking powder*	2 *egg whites*

Preheat the oven to 350°F. Spray nonstick muffin tins with nonstick vegetable cooking spray and set aside.

In a large bowl, combine the sweet potato, flour, sugar, raisins, nuts, baking powder, cinnamon, nutmeg and salt, mixing well. In a separate bowl, beat together the milk, margarine and egg whites with a wire whisk. Slowly add the milk mixture to the other ingredients, stirring well with a fork just until the dry ingredients are mixed. Do not overmix.

Fill each muffin tin two-thirds full with batter. Bake for 30 minutes, or until a cake tester inserted into the muffins comes out clean. Remove the muffins from the pan immediately and serve hot.

PER MUFFIN	KCAL	FATgm	CHOLmg	SODmg
	82	3	1	42

JALAPENO CORNBREAD

MAKES 8 SERVINGS

THIS SPICY CORNBREAD is great as a side dish, and it's terrific for stuffings and dressing mixes.

1 *cup yellow cornmeal*
½ *cup all-purpose flour*
1 *teaspoon baking*
  powder
½ *teaspoon salt*
½ *cup evaporated skim*
  milk

½ *cup water*
1 *tablespoon reduced-*
  calorie margarine
2 *medium jalapeño*
  peppers, finely
  chopped
1 *egg*

Preheat the oven to 350°F. Spray a 9-inch baking dish with nonstick vegetable cooking spray and set aside.

In a medium bowl, combine the cornmeal, flour, baking powder and salt; set aside. In a small bowl, combine the milk, water, margarine, jalapeños and egg and beat with a wire whisk. Add the milk mixture to the dry ingredients and mix well.

Pour the batter into the prepared pan. Bake for 30 minutes, or until golden brown. Serve hot.

PER SERVING	KCAL	FATgm	CHOLmg	SODmg
	103	2	35	290

APPLE BREAD

MAKES 6 SERVINGS

1 egg plus 2 egg whites
½ cup sugar
1 tablespoon reduced-calorie margarine, melted
1 cup whole wheat flour
½ teaspoon baking soda

½ teaspoon ground nutmeg
¼ teaspoon salt
½ teaspoon vanilla extract
2 cups peeled and chopped apples

Preheat the oven to 350°F. Spray a 9-by-5-by-3-inch loaf pan with nonstick vegetable cooking spray and set aside.

In the large bowl of an electric mixer, combine the egg and egg whites; beat them on medium speed, gradually adding the sugar, until fluffy. Beat in the margarine, stopping the mixture occasionally to scrape down the sides of the bowl.

In a separate bowl, sift together the flour, baking soda, nutmeg and salt. Gradually add to the egg mixture along with the vanilla and apples, mix well. Pour the batter into the prepared loaf pan.

Bake for 30 minutes, or until a toothpick or cake tester inserted near the middle comes out clean. Let cool for 10 minutes, then cool the bread on a wire rack for 30 minutes before slicing.

PER SERVING	KCAL	FATgm	CHOLmg	SODmg
	166	2	46	201

DESSERTS

SPICED PEARS

MAKES 2 SERVINGS

*J*THESE PEARS can be eaten alone, but are even better with a slice of angel food cake. The pears will keep for several weeks in the refrigerator if placed in a tightly covered sterilized jar.

4 *medium pears, peeled,*
   cored and quartered
8 *whole cloves*
½ *cup water*

¼ *cup sugar*
¼ *cup balsamic vinegar*
1 *cinnamon stick*

Insert the cloves into 8 of the pear quarters; set aside. In a large saucepan, combine the water, sugar, vinegar and cinnamon stick, and bring to a boil. Add the pears; and simmer, covered, for 30 minutes, or until the sauce thickens, stirring often. Serve hot.

PER SERVING	KCAL	FATgm	CHOLmg	SODmg
	198	1	0	7

PRUDHOMME FAMILY FRUIT SALAD

MAKES 4 SERVINGS

WHEN I WAS A CHILD, we had a delicious fruit salad for dessert every Christmas, New Year's and Easter. When I had children of my own, we had fruit salad every Sunday. The kids loved this dish, and as they grew and got married, I always sent them home with a jarful to enjoy later. Although I have always had a fondness for this dessert, I didn't need all those extra calories, so I've altered the recipe for a low-calorie version.

1 cup seedless grapes
1 cup sliced banana
1 cup diced orange
  sections
One 8-ounce can fruit
  cocktail (no sugar
  added)

1 cup diced apple
1 cup evaporated skim
  milk
3 packets sugar substitute

In a large mixing bowl, combine all the ingredients, mixing well. Chill until ready to serve.

PER SERVING	KCAL	FATgm	CHOLmg	SODmg
	149	0.5	3	78

APPLE LOVER'S DREAM

MAKES 4 SERVINGS

I PREPARED THIS DISH for a favorite customer of mine who has a real sweet tooth.

4 **medium apples, cored**
1 **cup water**
½ **cup raisins**
1 **tablespoon balsamic
    vinegar**

1 **tablespoon Frangelico
    liqueur (optional)**
1 **teaspoon brown sugar
    substitute**
2 **teaspoons cornstarch**

Preheat the oven to 375°F.

Arrange the apples in an 8-inch-square baking dish and set aside.

In a blender, combine the water, raisins, vinegar, liqueur and sugar substitute and process until smooth. Stuff some of the mixture into the center of each apple, then pour the remaining mixture in the dish. Cover with aluminum foil and bake for 1 hour, or until the apples are tender. Remove from the oven, but do not discard the liquid. Place the apples on warm serving plates.

Place the reserved liquid in a small saucepan and add the cornstarch to dissolve. Bring to a boil; boil for 1 minute, or until the sauce thickens, stirring often. Remove from the heat and spoon over each apple.

PER SERVING	KCAL	FATgm	CHOLmg	SODmg
	147	0.5	0	5

STRAWBERRY DELIGHT

MAKES 2 SERVINGS

1 pint fresh strawberries
2 packets sugar substitute
*2 tablespoons coffee-
    flavored liqueur*

*⅛ teaspoon strawberry
    flavoring*
*Low-Fat Whipped Topping
    (recipe follows)*

Wash the strawberries and remove the stems. Place in food processor and process until coarsely chopped. Place in a medium bowl and sprinkle with the sugar substitute, liqueur and flavoring; mix well and chill. Spoon into 2 dessert dishes and top with whipped topping.

Low-Fat Whipped Topping

*⅓ cup evaporated skim
    milk*
*4 packets sugar
    substitute*

5 ice cubes
*⅛ teaspoon imitation
    butter flavoring*

In a blender, combine all the ingredients and blend at high speed for 1 minute, or until smooth. Chill well before serving.

PER SERVING	KCAL	FATgm	CHOLmg	SODmg
	114	1	2	64

PEACHES AND "CREAM" CHRISTEN

MAKES 3 SERVINGS

4 *medium peaches,*
peeled, pitted and
sliced
1 *cup water*
⅓ *cup reduced-calorie*
soft-style cream
cheese
2 *packets sugar*
substitute
½ *teaspoon brown sugar*
substitute

1 *teaspoon very finely*
chopped crystallized
ginger
½ *teaspoon cornstarch*
2 *tablespoons unflavored*
gelatin
½ *cup evaporated skim*
milk

In a 2-quart saucepan over medium heat, combine the peaches, water, cream cheese, sugar substitutes and ginger. Cook for 5 minutes, stirring often.

In a small bowl, dissolve the cornstarch and gelatin in the milk. Remove the peach mixture from the heat and stir in the dissolved cornstarch and gelatin; mix well.

Pour into 3 individual dessert dishes and chill for at least 2 hours before serving.

PER SERVING	KCAL	FATgm	CHOLmg	SODmg
	140	4	2	161

PEAR COBBLER SHERRY

MAKES 8 SERVINGS

THIS DISH is named for my granddaughter Sherry!

2 *medium Bartlett pears,*
peeled, cored and
thinly sliced
½ *cup water*
¼ *cup sugar*
1 *egg plus 2 egg whites*
2 *cups evaporated skim*
milk

½ *teaspoon salt*
⅛ *teaspoon vanilla*
extract
⅛ *teaspoon imitation*
butter flavoring
2 *cups quick-mixing*
flour
1 *teaspoon baking*
powder

Preheat the oven to 375°F.

In a medium saucepan over high heat, combine the pears, water and sugar. Cook for 15 minutes, then remove from the heat and set aside.

In a medium bowl, beat together the egg, egg whites, milk, salt and vanilla and butter flavoring. Combine the flour and baking powder; gradually add to the beaten mixture, mixing well.

Spray the inside of an 8-inch-square baking dish with nonstick vegetable cooking spray. Pour in half the batter and arrange the pears on top; pour on the remaining batter. Bake for 30 minutes, or until golden brown.

PER SERVING	KCAL	FATgm	CHOLmg	SODmg
	147	1	34	189

BREAD PUDDING WITH MERINGUE

MAKES 4 SERVINGS

WHEN I MADE this recipe, some of my grandkids were in the restaurant. After a few bites, they said, "Why did you make such a small one? I only had one piece."

1½ *cups evaporated skim milk*
1 *egg*
4 *slices stale bread (40 calories per slice), cut into ½-inch cubes*
5 *tablespoons sugar*
2 *tablespoons raisins*

¼ *teaspoon ground nutmeg*
¼ *teaspoon vanilla extract*
⅛ *teaspoon ground cinnamon*
1 *tablespoon reduced-calorie margarine*
2 *egg whites, at room temperature*

Preheat the oven to 375°F.

In a medium bowl, beat together the milk and egg. Add the bread cubes and let soak for 30 minutes. Stir in *3 tablespoons* of the sugar, the raisins, nutmeg, vanilla and cinnamon; stirring well. Spoon the mixture in an 8-inch-square baking dish that has been sprayed with nonstick vegetable cooking spray. Dot with the margarine and bake for 30 minutes, or until firm.

In the small bowl of an electric mixer, beat the egg whites at medium speed until foamy. Gradually add the remaining *2 tablespoons* sugar and beat for 1½ minutes, or until stiff peaks form. Spread the meringue over the pudding, sealing the edges. Return to the oven and bake for 2 minutes longer, or until lightly browned.

PER SERVING	KCAL	FATgm	CHOLmg	SODmg
	225	3	74	268

BEAU'S FRUITY RICE PUDDING

MAKES 4 SERVINGS

1 *cup evaporated skim milk*
¼ *cup sugar substitute*
1¼ *cups cooked rice*
⅛ *teaspoon salt*
One-half 8-ounce carton frozen egg substitute, thawed

½ *teaspoon vanilla extract*
One 8¼-ounce can mixed fruit (no sugar added)
3 *egg whites*
⅛ *teaspoon cream of tartar*

Preheat the oven to 400°F.

In a medium saucepan over high heat, combine ½ cup of the milk, ⅛ cup of the sugar substitute, the rice and salt. Cook, stirring, for 10 minutes, or until the mixture thickens. In a small bowl, combine the egg substitute, remaining ½ cup milk and the vanilla; stir until well mixed, then add to the saucepan. Reduce the heat to medium, add mixed fruit and cook for 1 minute, stirring often. Spoon the mixture into an 8-inch-square baking dish that has been sprayed with nonstick vegetable cooking spray; set aside.

In the medium bowl of an electric mixer, beat the egg whites at medium speed until foamy. Gradually add the remaining ⅛ cup sugar substitute and the cream of tartar; beat for about 1½ minutes, or until stiff peaks form. Spoon over the rice mixture and bake for 10 minutes, or until lightly browned.

PER SERVING	KCAL	FATgm	CHOLmg	SODmg
	184	3	3	231

PUMPKIN-PEAR PIE

MAKES 8 SERVINGS

2 *cups cooked fresh pumpkin*

3 *medium pears, peeled and thinly sliced*

1 *teaspoon brown sugar substitute*

¼ *teaspoon ground allspice*

¼ *teaspoon vanilla-nut flavoring*

1 *cup miniature marshmallows*

10 *ginger-snap cookies, finely crushed*

Preheat the oven to 350°F.

In a large saucepan over medium heat, combine the pumpkin and pears; cook for 10 minutes, stirring often. Add the sugar substitute, allspice, flavoring and ½ cup of the marshmallows; cook for 10 minutes, stirring often.

Spray the inside of a 9-inch pie plate with nonstick vegetable cooking spray (preferably butter-flavored). Add the crushed ginger snaps and spread evenly on the bottom of the plate, then spray again with cooking spray (this makes the pie crust moist). Spoon in the pumpkin mixture and top with the remaining ½ cup marshmallows. Bake for 15 minutes. Allow to cool before serving.

PER SERVING	KCAL	FATgm	CHOLmg	SODmg
	93	2	0	26

ANGEL FOOD CAKE

MAKES 6 SERVINGS

8 **egg whites, room temperature**
¾ **teaspoon cream of tartar**
⅛ **teaspoon salt**
1⅛ **cups sugar**

½ **teaspoon imitation butter flavoring**
½ **teaspoon imitation butter-nut flavoring**
¾ **cup cake flour**

Preheat the oven to 350°F.

In the large bowl of an electric mixer, beat the egg whites at medium speed for 2 minutes, or until foamy. Add the cream of tartar and salt. Increase the speed to high and add not more than ⅓ cup of the sugar at a time. Continue to beat on high for about 12 minutes, or until stiff peaks form.

Gently fold in the flavorings with a clean grease-free spatula. Sprinkle in the flour a little at a time, blending with a wire whisk. Pour into an ungreased 9-inch tube pan and bake for 30 minutes, or until the cake tests done. For best results, place on the lower rack of the oven and do not open door. Let cool at least 3 hours before removing from the pan.

PER SERVING	KCAL	FATgm	CHOLmg	SODmg
	200	0.1	0	149

FROZEN YOGURT ANGEL CAKE A LA JUDY

MAKES 8 SERVINGS

½ *Angel Food Cake (page 245)*
1 *cup low-fat soft-serve frozen vanilla yogurt*
1 *cup low-fat soft-serve frozen chocolate yogurt*

Cut the cake into six ½-inch-long wedges. Spray the inside of a 9-by-5-by-3-inch glass loaf pan with nonstick vegetable cooking spray. Arrange 2 *slices* of the cake on the bottom of the pan and layer with the vanilla yogurt. Repeat with 2 *slices* of cake, layering with the chocolate yogurt. Top with the remaining 2 *slices* of the cake. Cover with plastic wrap and freeze overnight.

Uncover and loosen the edges with a metal spatula. Transfer the cake to a platter and cut into eight 1-inch slices. Serve immediately.

PER SERVING	KCAL	FATgm	CHOLmg	SODmg
	11	0.5	0	57

SWEET POTATO CAKE

MAKES 8 SERVINGS

1 *egg plus 2 egg whites*
½ *cup evaporated skim milk*
2 *tablespoons reduced-calorie margarine, melted*
2 *teaspoons brown sugar substitute*
½ *teaspoon imitation vanilla and butter-nut flavoring*
1 *cup all-purpose flour*
2 *tablespoons pecan meal*
¼ *teaspoon baking powder*
¼ *teaspoon ground ginger*
¼ *teaspoon ground cinnamon*
⅛ *teaspoon salt*
⅛ *teaspoon ground nutmeg*
2 *cups peeled and finely shredded sweet potato (about 1 large)*
Creamy Pecan Icing (page 248)

Preheat the oven to 350°F.

In a large bowl, beat together the egg, egg whites, milk, margarine, sugar substitute and flavoring; set aside.

In a medium bowl, combine all the remaining ingredients; gradually add to the beaten mixture, mixing well. Pour the batter into a 9-inch cake pan that has been sprayed with nonstick vegetable cooking spray. Bake for 20 minutes, or until the cake tests done. Transfer to a plate and let cool to the touch. Top with creamy pecan icing.

PER SERVING	KCAL	FATgm	CHOLmg	SODmg
	108	3	35	147

CREAMY PECAN ICING

MAKES 1 CUP

THIS ICING is perfect for the Sweet-Potato Cake on page 247.

1 *cup low-fat cottage cheese*

½ *cup confectioner's sugar*

2 *tablespoons reduced-calorie soft-style cream cheese*

2 *tablespoons pecan meal*

⅛ *teaspoon imitation butter flavoring*

Place the cottage cheese in a blender and process until smooth; reserve 2 *tablespoons* (refrigerate the remaining cottage cheese for another use).

In a small bowl, combine the sugar, cream cheese, pecan meal, flavoring and the reserved blended cottage cheese; stir well.

PER TABLESPOON	KCAL	FATgm	CHOLmg	SODmg
	2	0.1	0.1	12

GRANNY CAKE I

MAKES 10 SERVINGS

1 *cup low-fat cottage
    cheese*
1 *cup sugar*
1 *egg plus 2 egg whites*
2 *cups cake flour*

1 *teaspoon baking soda*
1 *cup canned
    unsweetened crushed
    pineapple, drained*

Preheat the oven to 350°F.

Place the cottage cheese in a blender and process until smooth; set aside.

In a large bowl, combine the sugar, egg, egg whites and ½ cup of the blended cottage cheese. (Refrigerate the remaining cottage cheese for another use.) Beat for 1 minute. Combine the cake flour and baking soda, mixing well, then gradually add to the cottage cheese mixture along with the pineapple; beat well.

Spray the inside of an 8-inch fluted tube pan with nonstick vegetable cooking spray. Pour in the batter and bake for 30 minutes, or until the cake tests done. Serve warm or at room temperature.

PER SERVING	KCAL	FATgm	CHOLmg	SODmg
	75	1	28	147

GRANNY CAKE II

MAKES 10 SERVINGS

*J*I WAS EXPERIMENTING with different recipes in my test kitchen one afternoon, when my brother Calvin and his wife, Marie, came for a visit. This cake was ready to come out of the oven, so naturally Calvin and Marie would be my taste testers. Calvin said, "I refuse to move without this recipe." They loved it, and so will you!

1 *cup low-fat cottage cheese*
½ *cup sugar substitute*
1 *egg plus 2 egg whites*
¼ *teaspoon imitation butter flavoring*
2 *cups cake flour*

1 *teaspoon baking soda*
1 *cup canned unsweetened crushed pineapple, drained*
Stacie's Frosty Icing (page 251)

Preheat the oven to 350°F.

Place the cottage cheese in a blender and process until smooth; set aside.

In a large bowl, combine the sugar substitute, egg, egg whites, flavoring and ½ cup of the blended cottage cheese. (Refrigerate the remaining cottage cheese for another use.) Beat for 1 minute. Combine the cake flour and baking soda, mixing well, then gradually add to cottage cheese mixture along with the pineapple; beat well.

Spray the inside of an 8-inch fluted tube pan with nonstick vegetable cooking spray. Pour in the batter and bake for 30 minutes, or until the cake tests done. Top with icing when cool.

PER SERVING	KCAL	FATgm	CHOLmg	SODmg
	103	1	28	147

STACIE'S FROSTY ICING

MAKES 1 CUP

1 *cup low-fat cottage cheese*
½ *cup confectioner's sugar*
2 *tablespoons reduced-calorie soft-style cream cheese*

⅛ *teaspoon imitation vanilla and butter-nut flavoring*

Place the cottage cheese in a blender and process until smooth. Place ⅓ cup of the blended cottage cheese in a small bowl. (Refrigerate the remaining cottage cheese for another use.) Add the sugar, cream cheese and flavoring; mix well. Use to frost cakes and muffins.

PER TABLESPOON	KCAL	FATgm	CHOLmg	SODmg
	17	0.2	0.2	25

MARSHMALLOW KRISPIES TREATS

MAKES 12 SERVINGS

3 *cups miniature marshmallows*
2 *tablespoons reduced-calorie margarine*
5 *cups crisp rice cereal*

Combine the marshmallows and margarine in a small glass bowl. Place in a microwave oven on high setting for 2 minutes, or until melted.

Spray the inside of an 8-inch-square baking dish with nonstick vegetable cooking spray. Add the cereal and melted marshmallows, mixing well. Press the mixture firmly on the bottom with the back of a large spoon. Let stand for 5 minutes, or until cool to the touch, then cut into 2-inch squares.

PER SERVING	KCAL	FATgm	CHOLmg	SODmg
	60	1	0	109

INDEX

G

H

N

O

P

Q

R

S

T